Studies in Writing & Rhetoric

Studies in Writing & Rhetoric

In 1980 the Conference on College Composition and Communication established the Studies in Writing & Rhetoric (SWR) series as a forum for monograph-length arguments or presentations that engage general compositionists. SWR encourages extended essays or research reports addressing any issue in composition and rhetoric from any theoretical or research per-spective as long as the general significance to the field is clear. Previous SWR publications serve as models for prospective authors; in addition, contributors may propose alternate formats and agendas that inform or extend the field's current debates.

SWR is particularly interested in projects that connect the specific research site or theoretical framework to contemporary classroom and in-sti-tutional contexts of direct concern to compositionists across the nation. Such connections may come from several approaches, including cultural, theoretical, field-based, gendered, historical, and interdisciplinary. SWR especially encourages monographs by scholars early in their careers, by estab-lished scholars who wish to share an insight or exhortation with the field, and by scholars of color.

The SWR series editor and editorial board members are committed to working closely with prospective authors and offering significant developmental advice for encouraged manuscripts and prospectuses. Editorships rotate every five years. Prospective authors intending to submit a prospectus during the 2002 to 2007 editorial appointment should obtain submission guidelines from Robert Brooke, SWR editor, University of Nebraska–Lincoln, Department of English, P.O. Box 880337, 202 Andrews Hall, Lincoln, NE 68588-0337.

General inquiries may also be addressed to Sponsoring Editor, Studies in Writing & Rhetoric, Southern Illinois University Press, P.O. Box 3697, Carbondale, IL 62902-3697.

Writing with Authority

Writing with Authority

Students' Roles as Writers in Cross-National Perspective

David Foster

SOUTHERN ILLINOIS UNIVERSITY PRESS

Carbondale

Publication partially funded by a subvention grant from The Conference on College Composition and Communication of the National Council of Teachers of English.

Library of Congress Cataloging-in-Publication Data
  Foster, David, date.
  Writing with authority : students' roles as writers in cross-national perspective /
David Foster.
        p. cm. — (Studies in writing & rhetoric)
  Includes index.
    1. Academic writing—Cross-cultural studies. 2. Academic writing—Study
and teaching (Higher)—United States. 3. Academic writing—Study and teaching
(Higher)—Germany. 4. Rhetoric—Study and teaching (Higher)—United States.
5. Rhetoric—Study and teaching (Higher)—Germany.   I. Title. II Series.
P301.5.A27F67 2006
808.0071'1—dc22
ISBN-13: 978-0-8093-2707-2 (cloth : alk. paper)
ISBN-10: 0-8093-2707-4 (cloth : alk. paper)
ISBN-13: 978-0-8093-2708-9 (pbk. : alk. paper)
ISBN-10: 0-8093-2708-2 (pbk. : alk. paper)   2005032994

For Suzy, once again

Contents

List of Illustrations   xi

Preface   xiii

Acknowledgments   xxiii

1. Introduction   1

2. Studying Student Writers in Cross-National Contexts   29

3. The Work of Writing: Student Authorship Roles
   in Cross-National Perspective   60

4. Shaping Transformative Writers:
   Priorities for Change   110

5. Teaching Transformative Writing   131

6. Building Transformative Opportunities in
   Institutional Contexts   172

Works Cited   185

Index   191

Illustrations

Figure

2.1 Structure of the German Educational System   30

Tables

2.1 Case Study Student Pairs   47

3.1 Upper-Level History Students   78

3.2 Upper-Level Religious Studies Students   87

3.3 Writing Task Patterns in Cross-National Comparison   88

3.4 Writing Task Time Periods in Cross-National Comparison   89

3.5 Upper-Level History Text Features   99

3.6 Upper-Level Religious Studies Text Features   102

3.7 Writing Roles and Rhetorical Stances in Cross-National Comparison   102

Preface

Students' writing has long been a major preoccupation of American educators, students, and, increasingly, legislators and politicians who see it as a major index of the success of American education. This attention to writing has helped generate interest in students' development as writers in other national educational systems as well. How, and how well, students write is a matter requiring an international conversation. This book is intended to contribute to that conversation by comparing American and German students as writers and, as an outcome of this comparison, proposing changes in the way students and teachers connect writing and knowledge-making.

The research project that led to this book began as an attempt to understand student writers in a different educational system. It evolved into a riskier undertaking: an ongoing effort to compare how two different learning cultures—German and American—sponsor and shape the development of student writers as knowledge-makers. This comparison led, in turn, to a sustained reflection on how American students might be given fuller opportunities to connect writing and knowledge-making in their undergraduate studies. This project has, of course, been shaped by my experiences as a teacher in both American and German universities. While I have spent most of my life as a student, teacher, and researcher in American universities, I have had the good fortune to participate actively as a teacher and researcher in several German universities. That participation over several years' time has enabled me to work directly with many students as they learned and wrote in their academic settings. These memorable experiences do not make me an insider in the German system, but they have given me some insights in the traditions and practices that shape German students' growth as learners and writers. I offer this book in the spirit of cross-national understanding, and I am grateful for the collaboration of students and faculty in both educational systems who made the comparative efforts possible by readily sharing their work. Without the generosity of these students and teachers who so freely let me into their lives, there would have been no project and no book.

It is clear that Germany's educational system has been stretched and challenged in the reunification process. The educational system of West Germany became the dominant pattern after reunification, but historians do not see the traditional German university system nationwide as without fault. Charles S. Maier says that despite their national dominance, "the West German universities should hardly serve as unquestioned models; they were overcrowded, relied on huge lectures, provided insufficient faculty contact with students, and had amorphous curricula" (310). The same complaints, of course, are frequently lodged against universities in many countries, including those in the United States, and with the pervasive rise in postsecondary enrollments internationally, these problems have not diminished. Thus the German and American university systems, despite their differences in structure and traditions, share many of the challenges created by the democratization of educational access.

While there are important structural differences between the systems and differences in how German and American students are prepared as academic writers entering university (explained at length in chapters 1 and 2), there are also similarities that allow useful comparisons between them. An important difference is that, while the baccalaureate degree is the first American university degree, the first German degree is a master's or corresponding *Diplom,* and German students generally take more than five years to finish their studies. However, curriculum patterns in the humanities and social science disciplines are similar in both systems in the first through fourth years of study. Courses generally move from introductory to advanced levels of disciplinary focus in both postsecondary systems, beginning with general topic and period introductions and moving to more specific topic- and issue-based courses in later semesters. A growing command of disciplinary issues and complexities is expected in both systems. However, because German students enter university in particular disciplines, and because they do not face general education requirements, they settle into discipline-specific course work sooner than American students. German students thus face extensive writing challenges sooner than American students, especially in seminars that require them to learn specific disciplinary discourses and genre conventions. As the following chapters show, the demands of seminar writing tasks create important differences between German and American students' development as university writers.

Each case study presented here develops the student participant's academic writing history, then focuses on her or his participation in a writing-intensive, semester-long course whose activities are indicative of literacy practices in the discipline and institution. In the German case studies, these courses are seminars; in the American case studies, because not all departments offered seminars, courses range from introductory to upper-level courses in the disciplines. The differences among these settings will be accounted for as part of the broader range of institutional and systemic differences examined in this book. Naturalistic studies of student writers are inevitably pulled between conflicting goals: the need for broadness and inclusiveness against the need for manageability. It is a commonplace that one can look at only so many variables; while many elements might be at play, only the most important can reasonably be targeted. Assessing the interactive influences of various contextual elements, important as it is to a broad research perspective, is a challenge to which cross-cultural analysis is particularly suited by its power to bring assumptions and unspoken premises into view. Focusing on students' performances in specific courses within their institutional contexts and relying on the case study method of inquiry, this study seeks to balance the broad structures of students' learning/writing environments with the specific, lived experiences of individual student writers.

The goals of this book are to compare the work of student learner/writers in their institutional contexts and knowledge communities, identify some major differences in learning and writing development, and, based on this analysis, propose ways to help American undergraduates better connect writing and knowledge-making. In the cross-national part of the book, both the systemic structures and the discursive elements of undergraduate environments will be compared. Both are crucial in shaping students' agency as novice academic writers. It is important to track the interconnections among institutional structures, temporal patterns, and discursive settings in both national environments in this comparative inquiry. Social and academic traditions, institutional structures, elements of lived time and space, and curricular formations all play roles in the contours of students' growth as writers.

Chapter 1 argues that a broad perspective on students' writing development is essential for understanding the social systems within which learning and writing occur. Charles Bazerman says that "issues visible at the more immediate levels of writer" are "part of larger social systems" that require a "systemic view" to understand (37). In this perspective, selectivity in access to academic study is a key difference between German and American systems. Education in Germany is based on early selection for the academic track, into which roughly one-third of all German school students enter, most at eleven or twelve years of age. This compares with the approximately two-thirds of American high school graduates who go on to college or university and whose access to postsecondary education is mostly a matter of personal choice rather than system selectivity (Anweiler 40–41; Matheson et al. 36). These national differences in selection and access affect individual student goals and attitudes in complex ways that will be explored in the chapters that follow. In particular, German students must learn to manage an autonomy as learner/writers—conferred on them by the German university system—which sharply distinguishes their situations from those of American students. This distinction is particularly evident in early semesters of university study.

Indeed, an important issue for both systems is the kind of transition students experience as they move from high school to university. Students gaining university admission by writing acceptable examinations or by scoring well on SAT exams are by definition successful agents of school learning. But in the transition to university they must transform their agency as learner/writers, learning new roles as learners and writers. Instead of keeping to tightly regulated activities and time boundaries, students in both systems must adapt to less regulated institutional and social spaces and to more diverse social interactions and work with teachers embodying discourse communities with complex, unfamiliar expectations. American students' transitions from high school to college or university are very different from those of German students, or those of students in most other national systems. American students in the humanities and social sciences typically enter disciplinary study inconsistently and gradually in the first or second year of university. German students fully enter disciplinary communities when they begin university study. Breaking from the regulated patterns of high school, German university students must learn to choose the occasions, time frames, deadlines, physical sites, and working rhythms for their seminar writing projects. Thus in their pervasive, important seminar work, they face a demanding freedom as learner/writers very different from the American postsecondary system of deadline-driven, semester-bound rhythms. The autonomy assumed by German students in their seminar writing is a useful model for observing the effects of self-directed, self-sustaining freedom on novice academic writers.

Chapter 2 explores some theoretical perspectives on the interactions of learning/writers' activity and social/institutional structures. As Paul A. Prior suggests, "The assumption of agency, of the writer as author," must be scrutinized in any effort to "understand literate activity" (140). Anthony Giddens's "structuration theory" is particularly relevant in comparing students' agencies as writers in different educational environments. Giddens proposes that structures of educational systems and institutions do not exist independent of the "encounters" of the students and teachers in them but are embedded in the practices by which students gain success as learner/writers. Individual agency, argues Giddens in the *Constitution of Society,* is the capacity "to exercise power" in the context of social and institutional structures—to be "purposive," to "exercise some sort of power" reflexively (14). In this book, "agency" will be read as students' ability to learn and modify the institutional and disciplinary practices needed for success as writers. Students both use and alter "institutional goals and practices" in their own practices, says John Trimbur, so that they "*join* their productive labors to the institutions and social structures they live within" ("Agency" 287).

Chapter 2 also introduces the case study participants and institutions and outlines data collection methods. Ten case studies form the basis of this study, with five German students matched by discipline and level of study with five American students. Emphasis is given to students' and teachers' own constructions of their goals and practices. Learning/writing environments are reconstructed from interviews, observations, and materials evidencing students' and teachers' goals and practices, institutional materials, and ministry and system documentation. Analyses of students' writing histories and practices are drawn from interviews covering planning, composing, and revising activities; texts and related materials produced by students; my classroom observations; transcripts of interviews with school and university teachers; and institutional and ministry documents, curricular materials, and program and policy guidelines. The urban environments of each institution will be outlined—"Rhineland University" in the Rhineland region of Germany and "Midwestern University" in an American midwest urban area. The description will cover the range of programs and the demographics of student populations as well as differences in institutional size and centralization (the latter related to national system differences).

Comparing Students' Writing Cross-Nationally

Chapter 3 compares the roles of German and American students as writers in material and discursive perspectives. As agents acting in institutional time and space, students' activities are shaped by the material configurations of their environment—institutional schedules, time frames, and deadlines. Students' authorship roles are scrutinized in terms of their relationship to the temporal patterns of institutional life. Understanding key structures that shape identity and practice in institutional environments can illuminate "the socially defined roles of the novice writer," suggests Anne Beaufort (186). The tightly regulated deadline orientation of American undergraduate learning and writing contrasts sharply with the German pattern of independent, open-ended learning/writing activity—visible in patterns ranging from the scope of extended research/writing tasks to program completion periods.

Chapter 3 also compares students' writing practices in specific knowledge fields. Expectations embedded in disciplinary communities and institutional traditions are compared in terms of their impact on the attitudes, motives, and practices of students in both systems. These analyses suggest significant contrasts in German and American students' approaches to the connections between authorship and knowledge-making. For the German students, writing took shape as an intersubjective process in which the authorial voice emerges within an incorporative dynamic. The German students were well aware of their instructors' expectations for a multiperspective approach to their topics, entering ongoing conversations about issues and problems. American students, on the other hand, focused on building dominant individual viewpoints with limited attention to established or competing views on the issues. They saw little place for themselves in broader conversations about competing perspectives.

Students' Roles as Writers

Based on the cross-national comparisons of previous chapters, chapter 4 examines the roles of students writers in each national system. If students are expected to develop significant self-directed independence as novice writers—as German students are—they will respond to these expectations by learning the planning and writing practices that will enable them to complete extended writing tasks independently. If students are required to take final exams and complete several term papers all within a short time at the end of a semester, as American students are, then they will develop short-term planning and rapid, efficient text-production practices in response. For American undergraduates, a semester's work is a network of tasks bound by obligations for delivery at many points. Their planning and writing are shaped by the deadlines of papers, quizzes, reports, and exams. In this context, tasks are deadline- rather than goal-driven, and students tend to rely on short-burst planning and writing to produce required texts at demanded times. They may have difficulty sustaining reflective planning and revision processes, unless these processes are learned as part of a complex of intentions embedded in students' broader writing roles.

To address these issues affecting American student writers, teachers can help students develop independence and self-direction as writers and knowledge-makers. Chapter 4 proposes that American teachers build their expectations for student writers around these active principles:

- The need to shape students' capacity for consistent self-direction as writers and knowledge makers.
- The importance of helping students learn long-term planning and goal-setting.
- The importance of helping students learn cumulative, recursive task development.
- The need to challenge students to participate actively in communities of knowledge.

These priorities are implemented in the planning goals proposed in chapter 5.

Empowering Writing as Knowledge-Making

Chapter 5 proposes several planning goals for teachers seeking to help students develop self-directed, goal-driven practices as active participants in knowledge communities. Perhaps the biggest challenge for inexperienced academic writers is to learn the responsible use of freedom. American students are accustomed to receiving explicit instructions about planning and writing deadlines and paper lengths as they develop writing projects. Teachers are accustomed to ensuring that students fulfill course requirements by required deadlines, since the American system holds students to strict credit/grade point accounting and does not tolerate hesitation well. But the freedom to reconsider intentions, change goals, revise plans, and rework texts is an essential part of productive knowledge work, even though students may well hesitate, become confused, or remain indecisive as projects unfold. For these reasons, it is important for students to experience both choice and freedom in their roles as writers and knowledge-makers. Chapter 5 maintains that semester-long writing projects offer the best opportunities for students to shape long-term, self-directed goals as they develop their views in relation to others in a specific topic field. Such projects offer multiple occasions for reflection and change, enabling students to build new authorities as writers and knowledge-makers.

To accompany individual teachers' planning priorities, chapter 6 proposes several goals for change at the curricular or program level. These goals, focused on encouraging students' self-direction as writers and knowledge-makers, can augment the goals of programs already in place in many institutions, including writing-across-the-curriculum initiatives, learning-community programs, and service learning programs. The availability of variable-credit, seminar-like courses can be expanded within existing disciplines and programs to give students flexible opportunities to undertake self-directed writing projects in a variety of fields. Also, teachers in many disciplines can be encouraged to develop stronger expectations for goal-driven, self-directed writing tasks in courses they already teach, rewarding sustained, self-directed writing practices. Students can be encouraged to step into more demanding roles as writers and knowledge-makers, developing projects that reflect the responsibility required of experienced knowledge-community participants. Chapter 6 concludes with several guidelines encouraging these steps toward more challenging roles for students who write to make knowledge.

Acknowledgments

I would like to acknowledge the support given me for research and writing by the Drake University Research Fund, the Drake University Center for the Humanities, and the German American Fulbright Commission.

A portion of chapter 3 derives from my article "Temporal Patterns in Student Authority: A Cross-National Perspective," *RTE: Research in the Teaching of English*. Copyright 2004 by the National Council of Teachers of English. Reprinted with permission.

I want to thank Reiner Rohr of the German American Fulbright Commission for his unfailing courtesy and support during my stays in Germany. I am also grateful to Robert Brooke, editor of the Studies in Writing and Rhetoric series, for his encouragement and patience during the writing of this book.

I received help and encouragement at all stages of this project from many people in the United States and Germany. It is impossible to name them all, but I would particularly like to thank Deborah Brandt, Bruce Horner, Otto Kruse, Lienhard Legenhausen, Joseph Lenz, Min-Zhan Lu, Winfried Marotzki, Ulrich Mohr, Julius Redding, David Russell, and David Veeder.

Finally, I am deeply grateful to all the students and teachers in Germany and the United States who participated in the case studies on which this book is based. They shared their work and their lives with me with enormous generosity, often for extended periods of time, and though they are recognized only by pseudonyms in the book, they are its core and foundation. This book is theirs.

Writing with Authority

1 / Introduction

How students develop into successful writers at college or university is a crucial issue in any national educational system. This seems obvious to American educators accustomed to thinking about writing as a specific focus of teaching and study, but in some ways it is even more true in educational systems where writing is embedded in specific disciplinary study and seldom discussed as a separate issue. Students' writing is directly related to issues of educational access, institutional power relations, system goals, and students' roles within the larger society. The continued rise in numbers of university-bound students in most nations (including the United States) makes these issues more important than ever. However, one of the sharpest differences between the US educational system and those of most other countries is the role of writing in students' access to postsecondary study. In most other systems, writing plays a crucial and visible role in students' efforts to get into university. In the United States, although writing is a major element of study in high school and college, it has very little direct role in students' efforts to get *into* college.

Indeed, the American educational system seems bipolar when it comes to students' writing skills and writing instruction. There is widespread agreement—something close to a social contract—that writing ought to be a fundamental component of the educational process, a specific competence students should develop and display in courses dedicated to writing, as they move through the educational system. Yet there is also criticism of the unintended consequences of this focus on writing, with critics maintaining that composition courses decontextualize writing by separating it from knowledge-making contexts. The conflicts between these positions have led to a persistent national conversation about academic writing at all educational

1

levels, which in recent decades has resulted in significant changes in pedagogy and assessment of writing as well as broadened attention to writing across the curriculum. This conversation has become international as well, with schools and universities in many nations becoming increasingly attentive to their roles in students' development as writers. This book seeks to contribute to this discussion.

The Goals of This Book

In the following chapters, I will discuss some of the major issues in this conversation, drawing on a cross-national study of German and American student writers as a primary basis of reference. I will identify some crucial differences between German and American students' development as academic writers and relate these differences to the ways each national tradition connects learning and writing. While I will point out advantages and drawbacks of the German tradition for students as writers, I will focus primarily on what this cross-national comparison suggests about American students' roles and practices as academic writers. Then, based on these findings, I will propose altering the orientation of American undergraduate writing by integrating self-directed, goal-driven, knowledge-based writing fully into the undergraduate curriculum from the beginning of college study.

In the first three chapters, I will pose several questions based on cross-national perspectives about American undergraduates' development as academic writers. Some questions focus on systemic and structural issues. For example, what impact on undergraduate students' practices as writers does the deadline-driven American semester have? To what extent do American undergraduates connect their roles as writers with their participation in knowledge communities? And what effect does the pattern of deferred specialization governing American undergraduate education have on students' opportunities to write as active knowledge-makers in specific knowledge communities? Other questions relate to students' roles as writers. How are undergraduates challenged to learn the self-direction and long-term goal-setting characteristic of those who write as experienced knowledge-makers? How well do students adopt recursive, revision-based writing practices in their roles as writers in discipline-based knowledge contexts? And what opportunities do students have to learn the intersubjective roles necessary for knowledge construction in disciplinary communities? The answers I offer form the basis for chapters 4 through 6, where I propose that American undergraduate writers be systematically challenged to write as knowledge-makers in specific knowledge fields as early and as often as possible.

In those three chapters, I elaborate ways to strengthen undergraduates' roles as self-directed, goal-driven knowledge-makers in specific knowledge communities. I maintain that the writing associated with these roles should be

- self-directed and goal-driven;
- recursive and cumulative;
- enacted within communities of knowledgeable others;
- intersubjectively oriented.

I propose that American undergraduates should be expected to begin learning early in their study to connect their roles as writers with active participation in knowledge communities. I maintain that more such opportunities will enhance students' chances of learning active roles as independent, self-directed learner/writers, expanding the range of the undergraduate experience.

Learning and Writing in Cross-National Perspective

The educational systems of most developed countries feature a range of educational pathways for which students are differentially selected at some point in their school years. Students entering academic tracks begin writing examinations and papers in particular disciplines in high school and become apprentice learner/writers in disciplines at university much sooner than American students. In countries such as France, Germany, and China, high-stakes written examinations are decisive in determining students' access to universities (see Foster and Russell's *Writing and Learning in Cross-National Perspective*). These features give writing a dominant value in the educational destinies of individual students at crucial points in their progress through their educational systems. Germany's educational system includes most of these features and has had historical influence in shaping American higher education. For these reasons, the German system will serve in this study as the anchor for a comparison with the American system. In Germany the combination of access examinations and early research/writing in chosen disciplines makes writing the central and visible core of students' educational progress through high school and university.

In the United States, unlike most other systems, students' writing has only marginal impact in determining high school graduation, university admission, or access to further professional study. Multiple-choice tests play an important role in access decisions: the SAT, ACT, GRE, MEDCAT, LSAT, GMAT—all the familiar acronyms, requiring little or no writing. To be sure, the ACT and SAT exams have short writing components. And Advanced Placement courses available in many high schools do require nationally evaluated curriculum-based written examinations if students want college credit for them, but they are not essential to most admissions decisions and are taken only by a minority of college-bound students, according to Educational Testing Service records. Perhaps more telling, about half of American states require some form of literacy testing for high school students (and some for college/university students also) prior to graduation (Educational Commission of the States). But unlike the tests in other national systems, these writing samples are not intended to measure students' knowledge. They are not culminations of repeated writing experiences in particular areas of study. Rather, they are intended to assess basic competencies, including writing, so that students can be declared graduated and can apply for college or university. Political pressures and competition for funds have made such exit tests and the writing samples included in them necessary for schools' survival.

While extended, curriculum-based written examinations play only a marginal role in most American students' postsecondary access, they play a central role in German students' educational access and progress. What does this striking difference in the high-stakes outcomes of writing mean in terms of broader differences between American and German students' competencies as academic writers? Certainly American students write often in their high school and university studies, as the American students' writing histories cited in this book make clear. An important difference is that American students' knowledge-based writing is dispersed and personal rather than centralized and systemically decisive, a matter of individual grades and credits rather than crucial performances for graduation or admission to universities. American school and university students finish their papers, get their course grades, and go on to the next semester; their writing is parceled into their course work and expresses itself in their credits and grade point averages.[1] For the most part, when American students leave high school or university, their writing carries meaning only as personal archives in folders and boxes. It does not in itself gain them university access or a degree.

However, if the difference between German and American student writers were only a matter of high-stakes written examinations, there would be little to compare, because the American system has never placed such examinations in a determinative position in educational access. But there are other elements of the writing development of German students that differentiate it from that of their American counterparts. First, German students in most humanities and social science disciplines must begin taking seminars and writing extended discipline-based papers in their major areas of study from the beginning of university study. As apprentice learner/writers in particular disciplines, they must immediately begin learning the knowledge-building strategies, genres, and discursive practices of their knowledge fields. Second, German students must learn to manage extended learning/writing projects on their own, outside the semester time periods that control American students' learning/writing activities. To meet this challenge, they must develop a purposive autonomy based on self-directed, long-term planning and writing masteries. These differences in material and social environments, the timing of disciplinary entry, and general learning/writing patterns all offer useful windows for cross-cultural comparison.

Studying Learning/Writing Across Cultures

What, then, might a cross-national look at students' learning/writing development in their institutional contexts have to offer? Cross-national study has the effect of making issues visible that are normally taken as givens, placing the familiar in new perspectives. Institutional and systemic expectations, learning/writing patterns, and students' roles as writers appear differently when compared across national contexts. The comparison of the learning/writing practices of American students with those of German students, who face different expectations and develop different authorship roles, will bring out a number of issues:

- How does American students' delayed entry into disciplinary knowledge communities compare with German students' early entry into such communities?

- What institutional and curricular spaces does writing itself occupy in the different environments?

- What differences in students' attitudes about writing and learning emerge between the two environments?

- How do differences in institutional expectations affect students' motives as writers?

- What differences in students' freedom and self-direction as writers emerge between the two environments?

Goals and Methods of the Cross-National Comparison

To explore these questions, the chapters 2 and 3 offer a case study–based, cross-national comparison of the writing of five pairs of first-degree students in two universities, one German ("Rhineland University") and one American ("Midwestern University"). The students represent four disciplines: history, political science, religious studies, and English/journalism. The students are matched at specific levels of study in these disciplines in both institutions. Chapter 2 offers a detailed explanation of the structure and methods of the case studies. These studies strive for thoroughness and specificity in the presentation of each student in her or his institutional/cultural situation. However, the goal is not to demonstrate that these students and institutions typify the diverse populations of all American and German students and institutions. Rather, the goal is to illuminate significant elements of each system by means of specific, situated case study comparisons and to establish connections among factors affecting students' agency and autonomy as learner/writers. The students' academic literacy experiences and practices, showing consistent similarities within each institution, provide grounds for the cross-cultural comparisons.

Germany and the United States have a shared history in higher education. The German university model was crucial in the evolution of American universities in the nineteenth century, as Laurence R. Vesey and Frederick Rudolph show. There are also shared structural and programmatic concerns between the two systems, discussed at length in works by Rudolph, Abraham Flexner, Daniel Fallon, Peter Windolf, David R. Russell, Mitchell G. Ash, and Helmut deRudder. The disciplines featured in these case studies—history, political science, religious studies, and English/journalism—have similar scholarly traditions and departmental organization in both universities, German and American. Classroom patterns are also similar in the courses on which these case studies are based, with class discussion and group work predominating. The most important differences are in basic system patterns: German students (like those in most other countries except the United States) enter university as majors in specific fields, and there are no undeclared or open-major students and no general education requirements to fulfill, as is the case with most American students in four-year institutions. Also, German students' work is not governed by the kind of structural regulations (credit hours, GPA rules) that force American students to complete course work by set deadlines. These differences will be extensively explored beginning in chapter 2 and will form the basis of comparisons of institutional structures, learning/writing roles and practices, and forms of agency characteristic of students in each institution.

Situating Cross-National Inquiry

In studying the interactions of learners and systems, says William F.

Hanks, "the hard question is *what kind of system, and what kind of structure?*" (17; original emphasis). Identifying underlying structures of each educational system is important in framing an inquiry into students' roles as learner/writers. Yet it is risky to study students' goals and practices as writers only by describing the general features of the system that shapes them. For example, summing up his ambitious cross-national comparisons of student writing based on school populations, Alan C. Purves says that his study was in one major respect a "failure" because general comparisons about student writing proved impossible:

> The construct that we call written composition must be seen in a cultural context and not considered a general cognitive capacity or activity. Even the consensus on goals and aims of writing instruction masks a variation both in ideology of teachers and in instructional practices. (199)

Complex differences among learning environments make general cross-national comparisons of student writing problematic. Specifically situated comparisons can better illustrate these differences as they emerge in the portraits of particular students in particular contexts. The connections between learning and writing are enacted by particular agents within particular environments. To bring structural comparisons into clear focus in this book, a detailed analysis will be made of students' writing activities and tasks, matched by discipline and academic level for each pair of case studies.

Student Writers in Comparative Perspective

In Germany as in the United States, school and university enrollment trends have accelerated in recent years. But German and American students experience the transition from high school to university differently. German students in the academic track have thirteen years of elementary/secondary schooling and are likely to be a year or two older than American students when they matriculate. In their final year of high school (*Gymnasium*), the students in this study focused on writing in specific disciplines as they prepared for their leaving examinations (the *Abitur*) to qualify for university admission. They entered university as majors in particular disciplinary areas and chose their courses in response to the requirements of these disciplines. In contrast, American students in this study took a variety of courses in high school, entered university in the framework of general education, and only gradually began taking courses in their major disciplines. In their composition and general education courses, they wrote short papers and exams in a variety of forms that did not require extensive planning or research. In contrast, the German students began writing in disciplinary seminars beginning in their first semester, negotiating the ambiguity and confusion of planning and writing lengthy research papers within wide, open-ended time frames. German and American students' development as academic writers in this study evolved from these general features of their educational systems, explored more fully in later chapters.

Teaching Writing as an American Tradition

The American educational scene has changed steadily in recent decades. The number of high school completers has nearly doubled in the period from 1960 to 2003, with almost 2,700,000 completers in 2003. The percentage of high school completers enrolling in college or university within twelve months of graduation has risen from 45 percent to 57 percent during the same period (National Center for Educational Statistics). This explosive increase in postsecondary enrollments has given the long-standing tradition of American composition a crucial role in the postsecondary curriculum. American freshmen are often pictured as unprepared for serious academic work and lacking the necessary academic literacy to succeed. For example, maintains Robert Paul Wolff, the first year of college provides a "transitional experience" for students away from home because they are not ready for the risky choices and freedoms of academic study (16). In most postsecondary institutions, this transitional experience consists of two components: composition and general education. Indeed, composition and general education are coeval in the evolution of American postsecondary education, as several historians of the English curriculum in American colleges and universities have pointed out. Writing instruction and rhetoric have been "a permanent and central part of the college curriculum" from the very beginning of American higher education, says James Berlin (2). In the process of blending older and newer traditions, the American preference for rhetorical and humanistic breadth strengthened in the nineteenth century, says Katherine Adams: "Students generally took liberal arts courses in their first two years," with the earlier emphasis on rhetoric remaining in the form of "two semesters of basic composition" (1).

The idea that students can develop a general writing competence in composition courses has been a major element of the American tradition. The goal of composition instruction in schools and universities, maintained H. W. Davis in 1930, consists in "mastering the principles of composition" and "guiding students to skill in the use of their living language" so that "playgrounds and campuses fairly bristle with approval for that good English" (799). An additional goal of composition, said Warren Taylor in 1938, is training in rhetoric for public discourse: "making reasoned evaluations of public utterances," assessing "lines of action designed to solve social problems," and giving voice to "the place of the educated in the electorate" (854). These goals have kept composition in a privileged place in American education and given support to underrepresented voices within the growing diversity of the American student population. With its unique blend of traditional and contemporary motives, the American commitment to students' writing as an explicit learning goal has served American students and institutions in important ways.

Longitudinal studies have demonstrated that composition courses can benefit students' early semesters of study (for example, Sternglass, Herrington and Curtis, and Carroll). These courses often introduce students to various genres of writing and can make them more aware of their roles as writers. Anne J. Herrington and Marcia Curtis, for example, found that early-semester writing courses helped both well-prepared and basic writers become more "confident" about their writing and develop a clearer sense of self-identity (271). Writing courses, says Lee Ann Carroll, create "situations in which students must consider different forms of writing for different, often complex, purposes and employ the kinds of writing strategies that enable them to complete challenging literacy tasks" (78). A clear focus on students' writing needs has also served progressive goals of student diversity in recent years. Expanding writing centers and tutorial programs are especially visible means by which institutions have widened support for underprepared students.

Yet despite the demonstrated impacts of general writing instruction, composition has inherited a divided and contradictory mission in American colleges and universities. American writing teachers juggle two pedagogical goals: they must teach writing as a specific mastery in composition courses while recognizing that students must learn to write as knowledge-makers in specific fields beyond composition. "In this setting," says Mike Rose,

> composition specialists must debate and defend and interminably evaluate what they do. And how untenable such activity becomes if the very terms of the defense undercut both the nature of writing and the teaching of writing, and exclude it in various metaphorical ways from the curriculum. (11)

Writing teachers must warrant the importance of treating writing as a distinct teaching focus because that is an institutional imperative and a crucial element of their professional identity. But so interwoven is composition in the basic fabric of American education—and so naturalized has it become within the American curriculum—that it is difficult to ask the question, "Why do we perceive writing as a separate learning competence requiring its own curricular space in early semesters, when students must eventually learn to write as situated knowledge-makers?" In this perspective, it seems logical to ask why students shouldn't learn to write as knowledge-makers in specific knowledge communities to begin with. Most of the educational systems in the world outside the United States do it this way, by developing their students as learner/writers in particular disciplines rather than as writers gaining a presumed general competence.

Opinion is divided on the value of teaching "general academic discourse" outside the forms and genres of specific disciplines. Peter

Elbow argues that a generalized academic style is sufficient for "giving reasons and evidence" and "clarifying claims" and is the best medium for inexperienced writers because they will learn "the intellectual tasks of academic discourse" while these tasks are "separated from [their] linguistic and stylistic conventions" ("Reflections" 154–61). He separates language-making from knowledge-making by maintaining that the "voice of academic discourse" will "seduce" students into learning only the "surface dimension" rather than "engage fully the intellectual task" (162). However, others argue that students can learn to write as knowledge-makers only by working directly in the contexts of specific disciplines. Russell maintains that "universal educated discourse"—what general writing courses claim to teach students—is "a widely held myth" essential to the institutional justification of general writing instruction. There is no general academic writing, no set of styles or genres shared by various academic disciplines. Rather, he argues, "disciplinary discourses vary immensely," with writing "appropriated and transformed by each activity system" in its own way ("Activity Theory" 60). Sharon Crowley connects the notion of a generic "academic discourse" with the composition tradition itself:

> Many academics still imagine that the academic essay exists, and I would argue that they do so precisely because there is a universal requirement in composition in which, they imagine, this universal discourse is taught. But this superdiscourse does not exist, and belief in it does not solve the paradox presented by a universal requirement in . . . composition. (28)

Crowley's dismissal of the idea of a generic "superdiscourse" is matched by calls for the abolition of general writing instruction by others like Joseph Petraglia, who maintains that students in composition courses "may have little or no intrinsic motivation to act as rhetors" (90–91). The conflicts between these two versions of writing in American academic settings—writing as a distinct competence, as opposed to writing as situated knowledge-making—have opened such terms as "writing competence" and "general academic writing" to persistent critique and controversy.

Whatever one's view of the idea of a general writing competence, it is clear that students pay a price as they move from general writing contexts into specific knowledge-field discourses. This price has been well demonstrated in situated empirical studies, including those of Barbara E. Walvoord and Lucille Parkinson McCarthy, McCarthy and Stephen M. Fishman, Stuart Greene, and Marilyn Sternglass. McCarthy and Fishman describe the complex epistemic transitions students must make as they negotiate "boundary conversations" by "preserving and contrasting . . . various discourses, moving back and forth among them" (422). Russell points out that "general education students are outsiders" when they begin course work in specific disciplines ("Where" 281). Obliged to write and learn as generalists in their early semesters, American undergraduates may experience prolonged life on the boundaries of disciplinary communities in later semesters.

Life on the Boundaries: General Education and Knowledge Communities

The tension between general writing instruction and writing in specific knowledge fields is intensified by the American tradition of deferring specialization while fulfilling general education requirements. A significant portion of enrolling students are undecided about their study interests in early semesters—an estimated 20 to 50 percent (Gordon 1). Yet even when they know their major interests, students' choices are typically driven by the demands of general education. In many colleges and universities—as at Midwestern University—general education requires students to choose from among a very broad array of one-semester, often introductory-level courses in a number of disciplines and fields, even though they may lack motive or desire for these choices. The curricular choices of the American students in this study manifest this generalizing tendency clearly. The stated goal of Midwestern's general education curriculum—"the breadth of knowledge and skills necessary to successfully function in a complex and rapidly changing world"—reflects the broad aspirations of American undergraduate education. At Midwestern, general education absorbs about one-third of the total number of credit hours required to graduate, and students take most of their general education courses in their first two years of study. This means that in those years, they will take a number of semester-long courses in various disciplines. In these courses, they find themselves consistently on the boundaries of specific communities, having to learn new terms, styles, and conventions as they read and write in each knowledge field.

General education offers advantages to which students in other national systems do not have access. It encourages students to sample a range of disciplines and their discourses with a freedom impossible in more discipline-specific university environments (like Germany's). It offers students introductory familiarity with the knowledge-making strategies of various fields of study. But students' experiences as writers tend to vary widely in general education courses. In her study of college writers in various disciplines, Carroll observes that "writing across the curriculum is a roller coaster with much writing in some semesters and little in others" (49). She notes that in some "introductory classes in general education, students especially value projects that mark points of transition . . . in which they are able to make connections between their writing and their own developing interests" (49). But for many students, the one- or two-semester experiences of general education requirements leave them with little experience of writing as knowledge-makers in specific fields.

The dominance of generalism as an American educational paradigm has brought about a debate about specialization itself, resulting in critiques of expertise as inherently exclusionary. In her study of academic literacy, for instance, Cheryl Geisler argues that the American system creates a "great divide" that grants some students access to disciplinary expertise while blocking others because professions "need other students to remain on the other side" of expertise, to preserve the power of disciplines and professions (230). A related argument is made by Gwen Gorzelsky, who maintains that public access to knowledge is blocked because knowledge professionals have "manufactured a hermetic professional discourse . . . [that] hamstrings our potential to participate in the variety of more public conversations we might productively enter" (315). What emerges is a "narrow, hierarchical professionalism" that opens expertise only to a "privileged few" (316). Indeed, concern for a "divide" between knowledge-community insiders and outsiders is a long-standing issue in American postsecondary education. The imputation of privilege associated with the "insider" status of those with academic expertise has long been an issue for American social critics. But it can be argued that connecting expertise with privilege is itself misdirected and harmful in undergraduate education because it turns students away from the institutional and instructional motivations that should draw them into active roles as writers and knowledge-makers. This issue will be explored more fully in chapter 4.

Overall, the demands of general education create clear disadvantages for students' development as academic writers. The writing tasks associated with the general education courses of the Midwestern students in this study exemplify general education's coverage imperative. At Midwestern, general education courses typically emphasize the significant issues, problems, and basic texts of disciplines. In the general education courses taken by students in this study, writing tasks emphasized students' personal analyses of these issues and texts. These tasks were often embedded in specific units of the course as a way of helping students learn each unit and maintain progress. This resulted in a pattern of short tasks of limited scope placed at specific intervals in course syllabuses. Such a pattern is appropriate for introductory learning needs, but it limits students' opportunities to explore disciplinary controversies in depth, master disciplinary methods of inquiry and argument, and incorporate a range of different positions within important disciplinary conversations. Seminars and other courses with extensive research/writing projects in contested areas of disciplines—those requiring immersion in disciplinary genres and discussions—are generally offered in later semesters of study, where they may be labeled "senior" or "capstone" experiences. In some disciplines, even senior students have little experience in extended research/writing projects in specific knowledge fields. As chapter 3 shows, the upper-level American students in this study reported feeling still on the edges of genuine disciplinary participation as they looked back on their undergraduate experiences.

As a result of this generalist tradition, American undergraduates often face an extended period of disciplinary outsiderness in their early college semesters. Even outspoken critics of American undergraduate education often accept the border status of undergraduates with regard to disciplinary participation. Indeed, they may share Wolff's belief that undergraduates need a "transitional experience" at the boundaries of several disciplines in order to have the chance to make "provisional commitments to styles of thought and action, to test them for fitting-ness" before they make permanent commitments to specific knowledge fields (16). But the provisional nature of early undergraduate semesters means that students are delayed in developing the habits and practices of active knowledge-community participation. In a longitudinal study of students' development as learner/writers in their chosen disciplines, Sternglass discovered that underprepared students had difficulties in meeting institutional writing "assessment" and "proficiency" standards and made little progress as writers in first-year composition courses. McCarthy and Fishman note how two students participating in their study of students learning to write in an introductory philosophy course struggled with "boundary conversations that scared Ginny to death and frustrated David to the point of anger" (445). These struggles can intensify for students as they enter major studies and take on more active learning/writing roles in specific knowledge communities in later undergraduate semesters. For many students, like those in this study, the pattern of limited-scope tasks produced in deadline-driven sequence (structurally suited to introductory study) can persist in the learning/writing work of major studies, when they undertake more research-based, long-term tasks that require immersion experiences. The experienced American students in this study acknowledged the characteristic habits of short-burst composing and the construction of single, dominant authorial standpoints in their authorship roles.

This evidence suggests that American undergraduates may find it difficult, when the challenge comes, to participate in disciplinary conversations, to connect their views with others in or across disciplines, or to relate their own views to the ways knowledge is constructed in specific communities. Such difficulties may block the synergism between writing and knowledge-making essential to students' full participation in knowledge communities. It will help now to look at these effects from a different perspective by comparing the American system with Germany's.

Learning and Writing in the German Tradition

In Germany, postsecondary academic education (as opposed to vocational/professional training) has historically been limited to students selected in earlier school years for *Gymnasium*, the type of secondary school traditionally leading to university. However, tradition is now being rapidly transformed as students seek widened postsecondary access. Over the last few decades, the percentage of German students entering *Gymnasium* has been increasing rapidly. In 1960, only about 8 percent of school students were enrolled in *Gymnasium* in preparation for university; in 1992, about 30 percent of elementary pupils moved into the *Gymnasium* track, with that trend continuing. Recent figures suggest that over one-third of German school students now graduate from a *Gymnasium* or other kind of school with an *Abitur* (Anweiler 53–54; Führ 257–58). There is also more flexibility now for students initially placed in a nonacademic track to cross over into the academic track, part of a broad shift toward more academic and professional education in Germany. This figure may be compared with the roughly three-fifths of American high school students who go on to college or university (National Center for Educational Statistics). However, it is important to note that American students come mostly from public high schools, a much broader, less restricted student population than that represented by the selective groups working in the *Gymnasium* track in Germany.

Despite the continuing growth in numbers of students seeking academic study, German educators do not hesitate to say that there is a traditional "German system of education" across unified Germany today. All children attend the first four or five years of elementary school together. But a major choice of further schooling is made at the end of the elementary period, after the fourth year in most states. Students (at the age of ten or eleven), parents, and teachers must together choose from three main options for secondary education: general schooling coupled with practical vocational training (*Hauptschule*), intermediate general schooling with advanced vocational training (*Realschule*), and advanced schooling (*Gymnasium*). A *Gymnasium* education is the most common pathway to university, though students can also win admission to university with additional study and successful completion of examinations. The numbers of students in all types of secondary schooling have steadily risen in recent decades, while schooling choices have markedly shifted, as indicated by the increase in the percentage of students entering the *Gymnasium* track at the end of elementary schooling. This trend indicates the growing importance of an advanced secondary education leading to university for many German students. Admission to university, however, is based on successful completion of the *Abitur*, which consists of examinations in subjects studied in students' upper secondary semesters. Students in most humanities and social sciences fields can attend the university of their choice if they pass.

German and American students' experiences of the transition from high school to university share some similarities but reveal important differences. In both systems, the regular reinforcements of high school—the daily interactions of friends and teachers within a familiar classroom setting, the intensive regulation of time and space—change in the transition to university. However, at matriculation, German students face challenges different in both kind and immediacy from those of American students. For American students, systematic regulation remains strong: undergraduate classes meet two or three times weekly, learning/writing rhythms and deadlines are controlled by semester limits, and grade and credit calculations are locked into semester credit/grade point outcomes. German students, on the other hand, confront a radical new freedom in their university roles. They must develop a new situational authority to deal with the challenging material and institutional freedoms of the university environment, and they must quickly develop a rhetorical authority adapted to the discourses of chosen disciplinary communities. These forms of authority are reciprocal and interconnected; both must be mastered together for success at university. They are responses to a structural openness in the university environment unknown to American students.

When they enter college or university, American students face different learning/writing expectations and tasks than do their counterparts in German universities. Primary differences lie in the nature, degree, and timing of disciplinary participation and in the writing tasks characteristic of early university semesters. These differences will be discussed briefly in general and then elaborated specifically in cross-national comparisons of students in their respective disciplines. American students typically begin with general education courses and general writing instruction. The American students in this study entered specific disciplinary study only in small steps—perhaps one or two courses per semester in freshman and sophomore year. The majority of courses in the early semesters are in the general education program rather than in specific disciplines. In contrast, German students—like students in most other European systems—fully enter disciplinary communities in their first year of university. They must write extended papers in seminars beginning in their first semester, planning and writing lengthy research papers within wide, often ambiguous time frames.

German university students' relationship to the curriculum and the institution is more undirected than in *Gymnasium*. There are general federal guidelines for completing courses of study within a certain number of years, but the students in this study give evidence that these guidelines are not enforced by the universities themselves in many instances.[2] German students can attend a class, listen to instruction, take notes, and participate in discussion without earning credit, or they can attend and earn credit by taking a test or writing a paper. Students in the humanities and social sciences typically enroll in several lecture courses and seminars each semester, knowing they will not complete them all for credit. They may stop attending some courses, since the university imposes no penalty. If they do not take the final examination in a lecture course or write the term paper in a seminar, for example, they simply get no credit and must re-enroll in the same or a similar course later—if it is a requirement they have to fulfill. The university is concerned only that they complete requirements in the right sequence. Nor does the university in this study keep the kinds of records found in American universities—summaries of courses taken, attempted, passed or failed, or left incomplete. Only students themselves keep a cumulative record of the credits they earn each semester.[3]

This autonomous condition is a new form of subjectivity for German students. At first glance, it offers all the attractions that young people hunger for: independence, the absence of daily control, regulation so vague and distant as to be effectively ignored—a consummation devoutly wished for by all frustrated teenagers. The difference is that unlike American students, who in the transition to college or university exchange one closely regulated environment for another nearly as controlled, German students suddenly discover that they are free in wholly new ways. There are no looming writing timetables, no requirement to finish any course they've enrolled in or else suffer consequences, no frequent interaction with teachers or classes to prepare for (courses generally meet once weekly). The students in this study generally view their efforts to seek a degree as a long-term commitment that they themselves ought to control, not universities or politicians. This understanding of students' autonomy as degree candidates is clearly inscribed in Rhineland University's institutional policies and practices.

Seminars in particular—in which students typically must produce an extensive research paper—confront students with a risky freedom. To produce a paper, students must make a series of choices fraught with consequences: students may choose not to write (thus deferring the completion of requirements), to begin a paper but not to finish (thus expending time and energy without gaining official credit), or to finish and submit for credit (thus setting a long-term writing task for themselves). If they receive credit but a low grade, they may choose not to ask the instructor to sign the credit form but request permission to write the paper again, or simply to give up and retake the course later.

In developing their roles as seminar writers, they must learn to use an incorporative rhetoric synthesizing the authoritative voices and perspectives of their disciplinary discourses. The rhetorical authority students must learn at university is grounded in *wissenschaftliches Schreiben*, which is best translated as "academic writing" (Brauer). The phrase, used by every German student and professor in this study and elaborated in many widely available German handbooks, suggests an essentialized and normative academic style universally accepted in German educational culture. Its companion phrase, *wissenschaftliche Arbeit*, connotes the work of systematic academic knowledge-building. This construct is universally accepted in German academic circles, unlike its American counterpart "academic writing," which has received widespread criticism in American composition discussions. As Lienhard Legenhausen suggests, the learning relationship between students and university teachers is based in part on the tradition of *forschendes Lernen* (research-oriented learning), which implies learning arising from participation "in the same research undertaking." This tradition asserts that students and teachers should see themselves as working together, collaborating in specific knowledge fields from the outset of their studies. For German students and faculty alike, the tradition of *Wissenschaft* signifies the systematic study of established knowledge about a disciplinary topic—which requires students to learn how to incorporate what Tiane Donahue calls "the authorities of the already-spoken" into their own developing perspectives (182). The implications of this tradition for German students' writing at university will be more fully explored in chapter 3.

German students must learn not only the rhetorical strategies of academic discourse but also new institutional roles and time/space orientations. The structured, teacher-centered environment of the *Gymnasium* gives way in university to the scattered resource networks, more distant instructors, confusing layers of bureaucracy, and dispersed academic units characteristic of university environments. Students must learn to work within new institutional and material spaces and accommodate a new time frame—based on wide freedom and autonomy—for planning, research, and composing activities. If students are to learn and write successfully within this new environment, they must build an independence unknown to American university students as well as new habits and attitudes as writers, especially the habits of self-directed, long-term goal-setting for planning and writing.

Thus, German students entering university must learn a new kind of independence. "Autonomy" is the term that has come to express this condition in the German academic tradition. Influentially articulated by Alexander von Humboldt and other educational reformers in the early nineteenth century, the idea of autonomy expresses both individual and institutional freedoms, *Lernfreiheit* (freedom to learn) and *Lehrfreiheit* (freedom to teach), seen as twin conditions of true knowledge-building. As formulated in the early nineteenth century by the reformers, institutional autonomy was seen as necessary to protect institutionalized knowledge-making from political pressure (civil and ecclesiastical). Deeply implicated in this understanding of free institutions, says Thomas Ellwein, was the concept of autonomy for students and faculty, framed in Humboldt's terms as *"Einsamkeit und Freiheit* (solitude and freedom) extending widely over the field of thought" (116). Autonomy is thus defined as a form of sociocultural space necessary for students, teachers, and institutions engaged together in knowledge-making enterprises: it is, says Peter Fischer-Appelt, "an individual and social learning process" making knowledge-building possible "through the free interaction of devoted individuals" (11).

Autonomy in this sense does not mean detachment from the world nor a refusal to commit to ideas or actions but rather the freedom to shape one's ideas and actions in relation to other views and events: the impact of autonomy in learning, says Fischer-Appelt, is traditionally seen to be "the character's transformation into action . . . the process of connecting insight with action" (11). This ethical aspect of the German tradition of autonomy puts a special responsibility upon both teachers and students—with twenty-first-century hindsight, not always honored—to critique social and political power when necessary. This ethical element suggests an interesting parallel with the American argument that the academic study of composition provides rhetorical preparation for participation in public life. Both forms of cultural value placed on academic study and discourse suggest that agency and autonomy are more than simply curricular and disciplinary issues. Indeed, they bring into visibility often unexamined assumptions about role-playing and power relations in students' participation in institutional and social structures.

German students' freedom from the semester-by-semester regulation faced by American students is an important feature of their autonomy. Students must reach down into their own motivations and construct daily and weekly rhythms that match their goals and plans. They must develop new practices that may shape a future still vague and uncertain for many and begin to build the long-range motivations needed to succeed.

Different Roles, Different Agencies

Differences between American and German student cultures are visible in areas beyond students' daily learning/writing work. They can be identified clearly, for example, in the different kinds of student activism characteristic of each culture—which, in turn, illuminate students' agencies as learner/writers. American students are as influenced in their activist energies as in their curricular practices by the centrifugal, localizing impact of the American postsecondary system, with its decentralized organization and local controls. Like the writing American students do in college and university, their activism is typically dispersed and particularized, its outcomes limited to its immediate context. To be sure, American campus activism has responded to powerful national issues, as during the Vietnam War and its aftermath. But in the absence of a national crisis, and lacking a central educational and political establishment to confront, American students tend to organize their activism within local networks and organizations. Of course, national issues and events can stimulate activist responses at local levels. But what spurs collective action in American universities is far more often social and moral issues—race, gender, and sexual orientation—than government policies. A homophobic attack, a racist incident, a literacy program, even a campus/community cleanup may bring students to collective action, which generally expends itself within the setting where it begins. The activist commitments that energize American students—genuine and compelling as they are—remain specific to the diverse cultural geographies of American education. As with the localized, personal outcomes of American students' writing, their activism constructs its significance within limited spheres of local and specific institutional contexts.

There is an equally compelling correlation between German students' learning/writing activity and their activism. The outcome of the

Abitur for each student is national in that it determines nationwide access to universities. So also is German students' activism typically focused on national educational and political issues. While the origins of the student strike tradition in Germany lie deep in European history, an important element is students' sense of the national power inherent in their autonomy as students. This derives from their awareness of the privileged place established for university students by the selectivity of the educational/social contract itself. Student strikes are a systemic feature of German universities (as in many other national systems), occurring every few years as government policies affecting students come into question. These strikes directly confront government ministries, those institutions that students know hold the ultimate power over their lives. When strikes arise, students put into play the material and discursive masteries learned at university, networking and coordinating across regional and state lines to stage simultaneous events in state capitals across the country. What students fight hardest for (not surprisingly) are their own traditions of autonomy and well-being within the social whole. In strike actions, students bring the discourses of student resistance into play by forming "strike centers" and "strike cafés," printing strike literature, and making banners for marches through city streets. During a strike I witnessed in one university city, a student activist explained her commitment to change the government's social policies: "Our educational problems are only a manifestation of social problems," she said, "so we need to address social problems with our actions." The stimulus for this nationwide strike action was the federal government's effort to change funding formulas for university education and to encourage four-year degrees to shorten the time students spend at university. Students perceived this as a major threat to the German tradition of university study. Well-formatted, carefully printed leaflets asserted that "there IS enough money, it's just wrongly divided," "Germany Without Education Is Like Kuwait Without Oil," and "We Can Do Without This Government!" This student saw herself as part of a national collective whose interests are essential to the educational integrity of the country.

The symmetry between the forms of autonomy students practice as learner/writers and the social roles they enact is clear. In the chapters that follow, I will explore ways in which these roles are expressed in students' choices and decisions within their institutional contexts.

Authorship, Self-Direction, and Autonomy in Writing Development

Students' self-direction as learner/writers is an important issue in current discussions of American education, as Barry J. Zimmerman and Andrew S. Paulsen point out: "A primary goal of education from kindergarten through graduate school is to foster independent, self-motivated, self-regulated thinkers and learners" (13). American students' readiness for sustained, self-directed writing is a key aspect of this concern about self-regulation in their learning progress. In the comparisons developed in the following chapters, I use the term "autonomy" to identify this self-directedness in student writers, in part because of its significance for the German university students in the comparative study reported here. To establish the usefulness of the term as a definer in an American context, it will help to place it in the perspective of recent discussions of student authorship in academic writing. In these discussions, the notion of autonomy has been critiqued for its implication that a "self" exists only "in its private space, motivated only by its desires" (Faigley 231). In this critique, as Lester Faigley notes, the notion of student writers as "autonomous authors" implies resistance to "community" and its interactive, relational values. Autonomy is also critiqued in the context of subjectivity analysis. An assumption of "autonomous authorship" is seen as blocking recognition of the social in the development of students' agency as writers. If, says Bruce Horner, students believe they are engaged in "a 'pure' pursuit of knowledge" as autonomous authors, they will misunderstand the power of "social contingencies" and "institutional structure" to shape writing activity (242). In this perspective, students' impressions of autonomy appear as a distraction, preventing them from recognizing the social and material situatedness of their learning/writing activity.

But autonomy is itself a social construct defining a particular relationship between social structures and individual agents. As the following chapters will show, German university tradition posits autonomy as a necessary condition of participation in the ethos of academic study. In this tradition, one can say that participating in knowledge communities by means of autonomous knowledge-building practices is an interactive process wholly necessary to the production of knowledge. In this perspective, then, autonomy may be defined as self-direction and self-management in learning, signifying self-direction, freedom, and responsibility in knowledge-building. Autonomy has long been given a positive value, for example, in language-learning contexts. David Little argues that one of the defining features of language learning is "learners' willingness to take over responsibility for their own learning" in order to build "a wider practice of autonomy" in developing language mastery (19). In this perspective, autonomy does not imply an individualist perspective in which students view writing as a lone enterprise. Autonomy does not isolate or separate the individual from intersubjective connectedness. Indeed, it means understanding writing and knowledge-making precisely as intersubjective action, so that novice learner/writers perceive their tasks as requiring responsible, self-directed interaction with communities of knowledge-makers. It also suggests students' capacity to control the material pressures of the American semester environment, so that students can build practices supporting reflective, recursive writing and knowledge-making.

In the following chapters, then, I define autonomy and self-direction as students' capacity to direct their own progress as writers and knowledge-makers participating in specific knowledge communities. To explore the implications of this statement in a cross-national perspective, it will be important to look carefully at the institutional structures and traditions that shape students' work as writers and knowledge-makers. Such an inquiry can help us see the systemic basis of self-directed goal-setting, cumulative and recursive planning, and reflective composing/revising in students' development as academic writers. In the final section of this book, I will argue that these basic elements of successful learning and writing should be expected of undergraduates from the beginning of their studies. Encouraging these traits ought to be a systematic goal of American teachers and institutions, precisely because the American educational system is not inherently hospitable to them. As the evidence in the follow chapters shows, American students readily develop practices—short-range planning, limited task scope, and rapid, deadline-centered composing—that bring them success but that are inappropriate for genuine knowledge-community participation. I hope that the following pages will encourage American institutions and teachers to reconsider the value of autonomy as a significant part of students' development as writers and knowledge-makers.

I maintain, then, that from a cross-national perspective, American undergraduates enjoy notable advantages in their writing development but at the same time face difficulties in integrating their writing masteries with the activities of their knowledge communities. As a result, I propose that American undergraduates should be challenged to connect writing and knowledge-making as often as possible in as many curricular settings as possible. I state my thesis this way: *Undergraduates should learn how to write as knowledge-makers, developing the capacities for self-direction, long-term goal setting, and cumulative, recursive task development and writing.*

These goals are basic to the responsible exercise of freedom and autonomy in all knowledge communities. In the following chapters I will suggest strategies for teachers and planners that can help students achieve self-directed freedom as writers in active knowledge-making contexts.

Notes

1. A number of postsecondary institutions use portfolio evaluation to assess student writing progress, but such attention to students' cumulative writing history does not have determinative public implications in the way that extended written examinations do in most other educational systems. See Edward M. White, William D. Lutz, and Vera Kamusikiri on American portfolio evaluation.

2. This rule is currently under debate in federal and state governments, many academics and politicians arguing that it is high time to tighten up time requirements for degree completion.

3. It is the students' responsibility to present this record to the university when they petition to take comprehensive examinations and write the thesis for the master's degree. They must present a verifying document for each credit they

have received. Students keep these documents *(Leistungsnachweise)* uneasily in file folders and desk drawers; they must appear at the testing office *(Prüfungsamt)* clutching a sheaf of documents attesting to all the credits they have earned in order to prove their eligibility to write exams and theses.

2 / Studying Student Writers in Cross-National Contexts

German and American educational systems differ in selectivity, access, and disciplinary entry. Like many other systems outside the United States, the German system features both selection and choice for school students at earlier ages than in the American system. German students are generally selected for different educational pathways at the age of ten or eleven (students, their families, and school authorities collaborate in this process), and about one-third of these students enter the academic track at eleven or twelve years of age. Their academic studies are spread across a variety of subjects, but at the upper secondary level they narrow their focus to a few and must enter university as students of specific disciplines. This early selection process stands in clear contrast to the deferred selectivity and specialization of the American system, which makes various secondary and postsecondary options consistently available to American students throughout their schooling. Because of the range of options in American postsecondary education, students' access to postsecondary education is as much a matter of personal choice as of system selectivity. How these differences affect students' attitudes and goals as writers and knowledge-makers will be explored below and in later chapters.

Comparing Two Systems

Historically, education in Germany is based on early selectivity and differentiated goal-orientation (see figure 2.1). There are multiple pathways to vocations and degrees through varying lengths and outcomes of schooling (Golz and Mayrhofer; Führ; Anweiler). Those in the *Gymnasium* track must at the beginning of the final two *Gymnasium* years choose the subjects they will focus on in their *Abitur,* still two years away. In those two years, they undergo intensive preparation and re-hearsal for the examinations.[1] Thus the academic track in most German states takes thirteen years from elementary through *Gymnasium* levels, so students are at least nineteen years old when they leave *Gymnasium.* German men must serve a year in the army or in national service, normally before university, so most men are at least twenty years old when they enter university.

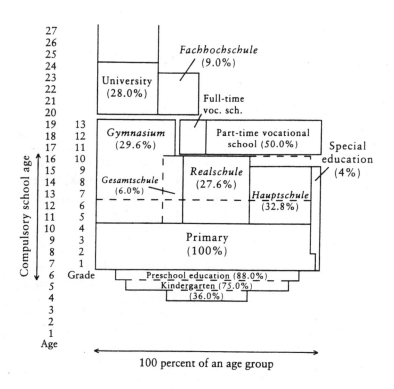

Fig. 2.1. The structure of the German educational system. Reprinted from *Internet Encyclopedia of National Systems of Education,* vol. 1, T. Neville Postlethwaite et al. (1995), with permission of Elsevier.

German High School Patterns

Because students wanting to go to university must, along with their families, make their choices relatively early in their school years, the selection decision is not an easy one for many families. The decision is not a top-down administrative process but a collaboration among students, parents, teachers, and administrators seeking a mutually agreeable decision. The children and their families must think a long way into the future, develop academic or vocational goals, and choose the appropriate schooling. A number of states require a trial period at the fifth- and sixth-grade levels, during which students have to prove an aptitude for studying in the type of school they have chosen. To be sure, students may change school types after the trial period or even at later points in their education, but they are required to "prove aptitude" to do so (Golz and Mayrhofer 22). Crossovers—for example, changing from a vocational to an academic track—are possible but require concerted effort and intensive goal-reformulation to accomplish. To qualify for university, students must first qualify for the academic school track and complete the *Abitur* as a culmination of their studies.

German students who are selected for *Gymnasium* spend six or seven years as part of a group of learners preparing themselves for one goal: passing the *Abitur* in order to qualify for university. The guidelines for courses at the senior high (*Oberstufe*) level assert close connections between learning and writing. The primary focus of all writing expectations is on students' preparation for the *Abitur,* which are essay-based in all humanities and social sciences. The guidelines state that the writing in each course must "verify the student's readiness for the *Abitur* and the general readiness for university. . . . Every *Oberstufe* course, including its forms of learning assessment, offers a systematic preparation for the *Abitur* examination" (*History* 100). The *Abitur* examinations consist of a series of written and oral tests extending over several days, taken usually during or after the final semester in *Gymnasium*. Students must write their *Abitur* exams in areas chosen at the beginning of the senior high studies. Thus the final year of secondary study is given over to intensive test preparation in specific subject areas. Indeed, test-preparation activity increases in frequency and intensity in the year leading up to the exams. When students receive a passing grade for their *Abitur,* they may choose to enroll at any university offering the major subjects they seek. In high-demand fields like medicine, law, and some sciences, enrollments are limited, but in most humanities and social sciences subjects, students with a successful *Abitur* will be able to enroll at nearly any university in the major they choose.

For American students, the linkage between high school and university courses in a given discipline is more contingent and less systematic than for German students. Some American students in this study had several high school courses in disciplines they later decided to major in; others had only the required high school minimums when they entered university. The unpredictability of this articulation between high school and university study means that unlike German students, American students are often newcomers to specific disciplines at college, having had little opportunity to develop interest in or familiarity with any particular knowledge field beyond general high school requirements.

Yet these differences do not mean that German students have smooth transitions to university study; indeed, the evidence of this study suggests just the opposite. Despite their disciplinary preparations, the German students in this study reported more dissonance and anxiety in the transition to university as writers than did the American students. They experienced a disjunction between school and university seminar writing. Their intensive preparation in test-writing for the *Abitur* did not prepare them for extended research/writing in seminars. In contrast, the American students in this study reported little difficulty in making the transition as writers because they felt that the variety of writing in high school prepared them for the various—mostly short—writing tasks in college composition and general education courses. In addition, the German students were challenged by the new autonomy they had to learn to negotiate as university students, especially in seminars. The sudden need to develop self-directed responsibility for their learning/writing work, especially in seminars, forced them to construct new forms of personal agency as learner/writers and to do this more sharply and quickly than the American students.

The Challenge of Autonomy: German Students

Both German and American students must acculturate themselves to new learning environments at university. For German students, the familiar activities of *Gymnasium* are gone—the daily interactions of friends and trusted teachers within a familiar classroom setting and the strong goal-orientation of *Abitur* preparation. Instead, German university students (like university students in most countries) must join classes with students whose backgrounds and goals diverge widely and work with teachers representing new, more stringent expectations. They encounter new expectations for autonomous learning and writing as part of the seminar tradition, entailing both freedom and responsibility. Enrolling in discipline-specific seminars early in their studies, German students are typically challenged to begin planning and developing extended seminar writing tasks in their first year.

However, their course selections require individual choices that the American system does not permit. That is, because German students may sit in courses and leave them at will, and because they may decide to complete course work or not without any systemic consequences like bad grades, students must make a series of choices during each semester. They must continually reenact a university version of building the house that Jack built: they must choose the course to pick the topic to write the paper to earn the credit to fulfill requirements in their major and minor studies. If they don't complete the work, the consequences are lost opportunities and the additional time and money it will cost them (or their families) to take the required work later. These complex personal choices define their roles as student writers throughout their studies.

Deferred Choices: American Students

American students in most humanities and social science programs develop program identity slowly in their early semesters because they must fulfill general education and general writing requirements. There is a distinct advantage to this pattern: American undergraduates have more flexibility and capacity for rethinking interests in the early semesters precisely because the wide range of general education requirements makes it difficult for them to invest deeply in major studies right away. But as later chapters will show, the price of this deferral of choice can be a sense of marginalization, which may keep students on the boundaries of genuine knowledge-community participation during these critical early semesters.

These characteristics of the American transition from high school to university have a significant impact on students' experiences as new writers at university, according to the students in this study. The American students reported little difficulty in making the transition as writers from high school to university and indicated feeling positive about their high school writing experiences when they entered university. The variety of writing tasks they faced in composition and general education courses in early university semesters—from argument and analysis to personal narrative—matched the range of their high school writing. Jill, from an urban public high school, said she had no difficulty in writing in introductory university history courses because her extensive high school preparation in argumentation—particularly in tight "five-paragraph essay" form—helped her shape her topics efficiently in the mostly short papers she wrote: "They were most like what I had done before [in high school]." Sarah's experience (coming from a small Catholic high school) was similar. In her third semester as a history major, she noted that she was schooled "to be a clear and concise writer," enabling her to "make an argument and stick to it, which is what you do in college." Because she had learned in school how to "focus on making your point" efficiently, she "wrote . . . in the way the teachers wanted" and earned good grades. Toni, also from a urban public high school, found that "the writing I did in high school gave me the understanding of the language . . . in representation, interpretation" that she needed in university writing, so that when she arrived at university, "I pretty much stuck with it. . . . It really helped there." In contrast, the German students in this study report that they entered the university without an understanding of the seminar writing tasks they would face or the strategies needed to accomplish them. Their test-oriented writing in high school did not prepare them for the writing work of seminars—developing the rhetorical masteries needed to shape their own perspectives amid the authoritative voices of their disciplines.

With this brief introduction to some important differences between school and university systems, it is necessary to describe the research contexts and methods of this study.

Studying Institutions and Students
Research Contexts

Comparing the work of writing and learning across cultures requires that this work be situated within its cultural contexts as fully as possible. A broad perspective on student writers and their contexts is developed through activity theory analysis. Drawing on Cole and Engeström's formulation of activity theory, Russell argues that writing must be studied as an element of an "activity system," an "ongoing, historically-conditioned, dialectally structured . . . human interaction" ("Rethinking Genre" 510). Russell views "context" holistically as an "ongoing accomplishment, not a container for actions or texts" (513). In Russell's view, the dancer cannot be separated from the dance: "The activity system [itself] is the basic unit of analysis" (510), so that any activity or text must be situated in relation to influences that shape it. Because systems are "dynamic" and context "ongoing," students' success as learner/writers may entail simultaneous masteries of various institutional practices, systems, and spaces. Prior's study of students' development as writers in specific contexts offers an example of this kind of study: "Representations of writing and expertise as activity need to be grounded in full accounts of literate activity" (150). Researchers, he says, need "to see persons and societies as co-constituted in streams of situated activity" (159). Prior examines American graduate students' participation in the learning/writing activities of seminars, focusing on text planning and production within their disciplinary communities. He also calls for more research "that might begin with the student, the cyclic activities of a day in the life," and would follow "specific artifacts, practices, and institutions" (272).

This attention to the immediate daily contexts of time and space in students' writing is explicitly developed by Elaine Chin in her study of the learning/writing experiences of journalism students. Chin notes that "relatively few studies have attended to the immediate, local impact that the culture of an institution or organization can have upon acts of writing" (451). She urges the importance of studying students as they "construct their contexts for writing through their lived experience in these contexts" (456). She portrays the physical spaces of hallways and classrooms and demonstrates the importance of "the ways in which writing involves both the bodily experience of occupying spaces and times that constitute the material world . . . [and] the meanings writers construct about what it means to inhabit such worlds" (477). Her analysis clarifies how institutional and disciplinary expectations may be instantiated in material structures and interpreted as motives and exigencies by students.

Support for a broad research perspective in learning/writing research also comes from "New Literacy Studies," a British-based movement focusing on what James P. Gee describes as "social and cultural (and . . . historical, political and economic) practices" of readers and writers (180). In this perspective, literacy is social practice, and discourse is social transaction. These studies have in common a relational understanding of literate activity, in which "people, environments . . . words, acts and symbols are linked to each other and dynamically interact with and on each other" (184). Because literate activity is embedded in social and cultural contexts, says Gee, text-making and discourse practices "have no meaning outside of all contexts" (188). Mary R. Lea and Brian V. Street have applied the situated literacy perspective to academic learning/writing, locating "student writing within institutional practices, power relations, and identities" (33). In this perspective, institutions are sites of "discourse and power" in which students construct and revise self-identities under the influence of changing settings and new social meanings and practices (35).

They point out that "a student's personal identity—who am I?—may be challenged by the forms of writing in different disciplines" so that "students may feel threatened and resistant," with cultural background, class, and personal ideology coming into play as elements of discourse activity (35). Learning to write successfully at university is not a matter of skills or even just socialization but of gaining the agency that enacts the expectations and conventions of knowledge communities.

Implementing the "New Literacy" approach to schooling, Street has identified important social and material constructs that bring the effects of schooled reading and writing into view. The intersections of home and school literacies shape "the construction of identity and personhood," which differ from culture to culture (128). Researching this interaction in an American school, Street gives special attention to the impact of material elements of school environment on reading/writing activities. Students are positioned by discourse "in a socially and authoritatively constructed" space and time setting, in which "the organization of texts, papers, and reading and writing materials" constitute "the organization of cultural time and space" (121). Street's analysis of institutional structures illuminates the semiosis of authority expressed in signs, posters, bells, and chair and table configurations, which shape students' literacy activities. This analysis is a compelling instance of a broad research perspective reconstructing social and material elements of an institutional learning/writing environment.

The literacy studies approach has illuminated the interactions of personal and institutional literacies as well. Romy Clark and Roz Ivanic describe "contexts of situation" as "the on-going web of interests, ideas, relationships, positionings, beliefs, values, plans, activities" in the life-worlds of subjects (64). They trace the planning/writing intentions of a student negotiating the intersection between her own strong views about sexual values and the traditional views of the academic department in which she was taking her degree. To preserve her own sense of self-image while observing the boundaries of institutional tolerance for "radical" views of sexual identity, she carefully limited her textual representation of resistance to received views of the "normal" (76). In such attention to the textual representation of the conflict between individual and communal values, literate activity can be shown to manifest the conflict and resistance found in the dynamics of social interaction.

Origins of the Case Studies

Studying students' writing development requires a scope broad enough to encompass unpredictable difference yet focused enough to offer an intelligible view of its subject. Qualitative study is particularly well suited for this purpose, since, as Robert E. Stake maintains, it is "distinguished by its emphasis on holistic treatment of phenomena," which "requires looking at a wide sweep of contexts: temporal and spatial, historical, political, economic, cultural, social, and personal" (43). For the research reported here, the case study method has been chosen as best suited to the qualitative study of learner/writers within different cultural contexts. The case study can achieve a balance between the individual and the social—between general institutional and social structures and the specific, lived experience of learner/writers. Issues for study will be, as Beverly J. Moss suggests, "context-dependent" and will "emerge from the social situation being studied" (157). While these case studies pay attention to a wide range of contextual elements—students' learning/writing backgrounds, institutional structures, disciplinary conventions, teachers' pedagogical practices—they focus on students' learning/writing work in one semester course in a particular discipline. The semester's writing work of five German students is thereby matched by discipline and by level of study with the semester's work of five American students.

Students' development as writers is based on many variables, some readily accessible to study and others not easily observed. In planning case studies of student writers, it is important to anticipate unexpected factors that may raise new issues and provoke new questions. To permit this responsiveness, asserts Stake, the case study must be flexible and open to "patterns of unanticipated as well as expected relationships," because many "situational conditions are not known in advance or controlled" (41). Such flexibility has been essential to this project as it has evolved. For example, as these case studies progressed, it became clear that German students' planning/writing chronologies for seminar papers varied widely, whereas American students' planning/writing times were uniformly controlled by semester deadlines. This unexpected variability required the foregrounding of issues not apparent in the beginning: the importance of time constructs in shaping students' relative agencies as learner/writers and the force of time and space variables in students' efforts to adapt to various forms of learning/writing autonomy.

How Sources Were Identified

These comparisons are based on five sets of paired student case studies focusing on students' writing in semester-long courses at matching levels of the same discipline. The German case studies are based on students' writing in disciplinary seminars. The American case studies are based on students' work in courses matched by discipline and level of study with the German seminars, but which in some cases are not seminars. Seminars are the only courses in German universities that typically require significant writing tasks rather than a single final examination. The German students in this study took at least one seminar each semester in each major discipline, which usually required an extended, research-oriented paper. At the American university in this study, seminars were not offered consistently at all levels in all disciplines. Rather, as at most American universities, students did a variety of writing tasks of different lengths, frequency, and scope in mid- and upper-level courses. Thus the variation in writing tasks among the students in this study is largely an expression of systemic differences in the ways writing and learning are linked in each university environment. These differences form the basis for the extended comparisons explored in the following sections.

Matches were made between pairs of students based on two variables: discipline and level of study (early or later semesters). No science or professional disciplines were included because of the large differences in institutional scope and resources between the two universities. German students were identified based on responses to invitations posted in departmental areas—the only feasible way of contacting potential participants at Rhineland University. American students were identified from lists of majors in each discipline, sorted by level of study, and randomly chosen for an invitation to participate. Academic achievement—in the American students' case, their grade point averages—was not known and not a factor. None of the participants were students in my courses.

The information and analysis resulting from these case studies draw from a variety of specific sources. "The important aspect of case study data is the use of multiple sources of evidence—converging on the same set of issues," says Robert K. Yin, writing of the importance of designing case studies to incorporate a variety of sources providing a holistic, wide-ranging sensitivity to contextual factors (*Applications* 32). These sources include:

- students' narratives of their own learning/writing backgrounds and practices shaped by school and university environments
- students' notes, journals, and writings
- course materials
- instructors' descriptions of their pedagogical goals and practices related to writing
- my observations of students' classroom and individual activities
- departmental, institutional, and ministry policies

Documentary Base

The documentary database emerging from these sources consists of the following:

- students' narrative histories of their learning/writing development covering senior high school and university semesters up to the case study semester (see appendix 2.1)
- students' personal journals of planning/composing/revising activities

- students' early and final drafts of their written texts
- interviews during the topic formation and planning phases in the case study semester (see appendix 2.2)
- final interviews for postsemester retrospective (see appendix 2.3)
- high school and university instructor interviews (see appendixes 2.4 and 2.5)
- my observation notes and summaries of classes in each case study featuring participating students' task-related activities
- course materials
- institutional and ministry curricular and planning documents

How Data Was Gathered and Analyzed

How information is gathered within a complex and dynamic field like writing activity is a crucial part of a case study design. The technique of triangulation—reliance on multiple sources of data collection—provides a means by which important situational factors can be identified and evaluated. Moss emphasizes the value of redundancy in identifying important but unanticipated factors in a case study: "Any patterns or impressions that the ethnographer recognizes . . . are tested by comparing one source of information with other sources," thereby "provid[ing] validity to data analysis" (160). To achieve these goals in this study, multiple sources of evidence provide the basis for the descriptions and analyses. This evidence reflects a naturalistic approach, with students', teachers', and policymakers' own constructions of their goals and practices as the primary focus of inquiry. Studying students and their writing, says Moss, "means opening up the research agenda to subjects, listening to their stories, and allowing them to actively participate" in the building of knowledge in the project (157).

In the study presented here, primary evidence of students' learning/writing goals and practices comes from their own descriptions of their educational backgrounds, literacy histories, and ongoing writing tasks and activities; from teachers' descriptions of their pedagogical goals and practices related to writing; and from my personal observations of classroom and individual activities. Systemic and institutional assumptions and expectations are constructed from these interviews and observations as well as from institutional, school district, and (in Germany) state educational ministry documents. Disciplinary conventions and practices are evidenced again from student and teacher interviews, my on-site observations, departmental and institutional materials and documentation, and students' notes, journals, and writings. Students' research, planning, and writing practices are constructed also from student and teacher interviews and students' notes, journals, and writings.

The interviews in this study followed the "semi-structured" pattern described by Stefan Aufenanger as "holding an open method to allow for circumstances" in an otherwise structured interview (39). A standard set of questions was asked of each student but were elaborated upon where additional information seemed necessary (see this chapter's appendixes for interview questions). German and American students' responses to each interview question were analyzed and compared in terms of topic categories and key words. Topic categories were related to the intent of each question and included instructor-student interactions, context awareness, topic formation, research goals, resource acquisition, resource analysis strategies, text planning strategies, and composing and revising practices. Key words were identified from recurrent terms in the transcripts, which provided the basis for analysis.

My Role as Observer/Participant

A crucial issue in case study research is the role of the observer/participant in the collection and interpretation of case study data. Case study researchers often build a close, interactive relationship with participants and their institutions, says Stake: "Qualitative case study is highly personal research. Persons studied are studied in depth. Researchers are encouraged to include their own personal perspectives in the interpretation" (135). What case study researchers seek is not distance nor detachment but the development of a holistic, personal interpretation of the evidence. Researchers can develop their evidence and construct their interpretations, says Moss, "only by immersing [themselves] in the community being studied" (157). The case studies in this book are based on my immersion in the activities and cultures of both universities.

My relationships with the American and German universities and students in this study developed in different ways. The American case studies, each lasting one semester, were conducted over several academic semesters beginning in the late 1990s at Midwestern University, to which I had ready and ongoing access. The case studies at Rhineland University had their origins in several visits beginning in the early 1990s, when I began interviewing students and faculty, observing classes, and collecting institutional materials. I made similar visits to other German universities during these periods as well. The case studies were conducted during the 1997–98 academic year while I was on a research/teaching appointment at Rhineland University.

Working in Two Languages

The task of bringing texts and conversations in two different languages into comparison couched in only one of those languages is risky but, I think, worthwhile for the cross-cultural perspectives it brings. All courses in the German case studies in this project were conducted in German—both course meetings and writings. All students' texts, as well as all course materials and institutional and ministry documents, are in German. When I quote German students' papers and documents in this study, I have translated them myself, doing my best to render the style and rhetorical structures of the original. On the other hand, the interviews with German students were conducted primarily in English, because most spoke colloquial English from years of study in school and abroad (and two were from bilingual family environments). Some of the instructors were also interviewed in English, but others, including several high school teachers, preferred German for their interviews. I conducted all interviews myself, in German and

English. However, because my spoken German is competent but non-native, those interviews I conducted in German were subsequently transcribed and translated into English transcripts by native speakers of German to ensure colloquial accuracy. The choice of language for interviews was in all cases made by the participants.

Implications of These Comparisons

The cross-national case studies reported here are intended to bring out important factors affecting the students' roles as writers in their disciplines and institutions. The students in these cases are not necessarily typical of the entire population of students in their system, nor are the institutions necessarily typical of all institutions in their systems. However, the contextual specificity of patterns and practices identified in the case studies is intended to give them suggestive weight. Individual practices may be taken as indicative of those called up by each sponsoring system. Students' practices are recurrent enough in each national set of case studies to suggest confidence in their reliability. Institutional patterns are indicative of those likely to be found in other institutions of their system. Not surprisingly, of course, students interpret their roles as writers and develop writing practices in specific, diverse ways, as the following analyses will show. From these analyses, patterns will be identified and brought into comparison, following the analytic strategy Yin calls "pattern-matching" (*Case Study* 106). The patterns of literacy development and writing practices are consistent within each national cluster of students, lending confidence to the comparisons based on them. These comparative patterns will serve as the basis for the proposals made in later chapters.

Case Study Institutions, Cities, and Students
The Case Study Institutions and Cities

Rhineland University, one of the two institutions at the center of this study, is a large university in a northwestern city north of the Ruhr industrial area not far from the Dutch border. Although not one of the oldest universities in Germany (it was established in the eighteenth century), it is now one of the largest because of the heavy population of the surrounding region and because it also draws from other German states and many other countries as well. It is selective in that, like all German universities, it accepts only students who have completed the *Abitur* successfully. The university has a wide range of programs in the humanities, social sciences, sciences, and professional areas at all levels including the master's degree (there is no bachelor's degree in the German system, though it has been proposed), other professional degrees, and doctorates. Its programs are housed in buildings spread across the city, semi-autonomous units within the larger university organization. Though its academic units are free to set their own curricular and research goals, Rhineland University (like other German universities) is subject to both state and federal laws and oversight in funding, overall program offerings, and faculty appointments. Professors, for example, are appointed through a national search process controlled by both state and federal education ministries. Students are admitted according to policies formulated at state and federal levels. Though this blend of autonomy and centralization may seem tricky to an outsider, university governance has developed in this way since the nineteenth century (see Fallon; Ellwein).

The city and its surroundings are white-collar and professional but packed with enough churches, castles, and historical sites to make it a major tourist center—"a city of churches and pubs, civil servants and students" in the words of the university's brochure. It is a university town where the bicycle is king: even though units and buildings are widely dispersed, students ride bicycles and buses to get around because traffic is limited in many areas of the city.

Midwestern University, located in a large American city, is a small, private, comprehensive university different from Rhineland University mainly in size. It is selective in admissions, with students mostly middle- to upper-middle class in family income and educational backgrounds. They come from midwestern urban areas like Chicago, Minneapolis, and St. Louis as well as from other major urban areas and several Asian countries. Midwestern has a range of undergraduate programs in humanities, social sciences, sciences, and professional areas, with master's and doctoral programs in several. Its colleges are tightly organized and administered, but (like most private American institutions) its funding, admissions, hiring, and program development are independent and regulated by the market in higher education. The campus is compact, with most buildings within walking distance of one another. The city is not a university town; it combines manufacturing, service, financial, and professional sectors. The car is king; the suburbs are expanding at the expense of the city, and students need cars to get to any activity not immediately connected with the campus.

The Case Study Students: Cross-National Profiles

Students in this study are matched in two categories—discipline and level of study—that provide a basis for comparisons in learning/writing histories and practices, writing goals and practices, and disciplinary participation (see table 2.1). The German students were all enrolled in the master's degree program in their disciplines—the first postsecondary degree in arts and sciences disciplines in German universities. The American students were enrolled in baccalaureate programs in the College of Arts and Sciences at their university. As indicated earlier, German students enter university as students in particular disciplines, but like American students they begin with general field and period introductions (though American students take a wider range of courses due to general education). Perhaps the most important curricular difference affecting students as writers is that German students write mostly in disciplinary seminars from the beginning of their studies, while American students' writing varies widely in scope and kind among disciplines and levels of study.

The four disciplines represented in this study—history, political science, religious studies, and English/journalism—comprise a balance of humanities and social science interests and a clear basis for matches between the two universities. Within the disciplinary categories, students were matched by levels of study, with three matches at the upper level and two at the lower level. The number of case studies was limited to five in each institution in order to make ample time for scheduling, interviewing, observation, document collection, and other activities essential to case studies. Students' levels of previous academic success were not known and played no part in the selection process. However, it should be noted that all participating students saw themselves as at least moderately successful, confident enough of their success to enter a demanding research partnership. It should also be noted that, though socioeconomic background was not an issue in this study, both German and American students described middle-class backgrounds from urban and suburban areas and schools. All students' names are pseudonyms.

Table 2.1 Case Study Student Pairs

Major	Rhineland University	Midwestern University
History (lower level)	Kirsten 3rd semester	Sarah 3rd semester
History (upper level)	Vera 7th semester	Jill 8th semester
Religious studies	Anja 6th semester	Mike 6th semester
Political science	Jana 1st semester	Kevin 3rd semester
English/journalism	Peter 9th semester	Toni 7th semester

The Students in History

Lower level of history—Rhineland University

Kirsten was in her third semester as a major in history, economics, and English when she participated in her case study in a history prose-minar (lower-level seminar) in the fall of 1998. Her home was in the university city; she attended *Gymnasium* in a nearby suburb and lived at home while attending the university. She grew up in a bilingual home. Her father is German, her mother American, and she spent two separate years in the United States, attending the fifth grade in Wisconsin and the eleventh grade in Houston, then finishing grades twelve and thirteen in Germany. Her father is an educator responsible for supervising teacher candidates in training. Her mother's native

English and her father's linguistic interests encouraged her to study English as an academic subject. In the *Oberstufe* years (last three years) of *Gymnasium* she concentrated in history, English, and French. Because she knew she wanted to go on to university, she studied hard in her courses and for the *Abitur* in order to have her choice of university, which a good *Abitur* record permits. She also wanted a good record in order to qualify for a scholarship from an independent source (in addition to the standard government benefits like train and bus passes and low-cost food). She chose Rhineland because of the strength of its programs in her major areas of interest. By the time her case study participation began in her third semester, she had completed seminar papers in three proseminars in her first two semesters at university, including one in history.

Lower level of history—Midwestern University

Sarah was in her third semester as a double major in history and political science when she participated in an introductory American history course in the fall of 2000. She grew up in a large city in Iowa. Unlike the other American students in this study, who graduated from public high schools, Sarah attended a Catholic high school, a moderately small school with about seventy students in her graduating class. Her mother worked in the county auditor's office and her father for the United Parcel Service. In high school, in addition to the general high school requirements, Sarah took both American and world history, each a year-long course, which meant she had taken four semesters of history when she graduated. She also took some journalism courses and wrote for the school newspaper, doing sports articles because she was a cheerleader and "knew what the score was" in writing about sporting events. But like Kirsten in Germany, Sarah recognized her interest in history in high school and decided then to major in it, sooner than most American students choose their major subjects. She served a year as a page and another year as a clerk in the Iowa House of Representatives and continued to work for the same legislator while studying at Midwestern. Indeed, it was partly to continue this job as a legislative clerk that led her to choose Midwestern and to think about working in the field of politics when she graduated.

Upper level of history—Rhineland University

Vera was in her seventh semester as a major in history and English when she participated in her case study in a history *Hauptseminar* (upper-level seminar) in the fall of 1997. Her home was in a small town about thirty kilometers from the university. Vera's grandparents immigrated to Germany from Poland, while her parents are native-born German. In *Gymnasium* she specialized in history, German, and English. She chose history, she said, because she had always liked the subject and because she had a very good teacher who encouraged her to select history at university. Vera chose Rhineland University because it was close to her home. By the time her case study participation began in her seventh semester, she had passed the exams admitting her to the advanced level of history study. She had already completed five seminar papers in history, three of them in proseminars taken in the first five semesters of study and two in upper-level seminars taken in the upper-level curriculum. She was also in the teacher-training program, studying to qualify for secondary teaching.

Upper level of history—Midwestern University

Jill was in her eighth semester as a history major when she participated in her case study in a senior seminar in history in the spring of 2000. She was from the Denver area and graduated from high school there. Her family had a considerable legacy of teaching: both parents were teachers. In high school, in addition to the general requirements for graduation, Jill took a number of Advanced Placement courses in various subjects, including two in history—AP American History and AP European History. She also took a number of AP English courses, wrote for her school newspaper, and wrote stories for herself about camping trips and vacations in early high school years. She chose to write exams for college credit in her AP courses and therefore wrote frequent practice tests for these examinations. At Midwestern she took a double major in history and English, continuing her interest in both subjects first established in her high school studies. At the time of her participation in the case study, Jill had taken twelve courses in history. But as she completed her undergraduate degree, she was unsure what professional goal she wanted to pursue.

The Students in Religious Studies
Rhineland University

Anja was in her sixth semester majoring in theology and English at Rhineland when she participated in her case study in a *Hauptseminar* in religious studies in the spring/summer semester of 1998. Her father was a clergyman in the Evangelical Church of Germany (Lutheran), her mother is a teacher of Latin and religion in *Gymnasium,* and her older sister is a kindergarten teacher. Anja lived in Mexico for five years when her father held a position there. She was also an exchange student in Australia in her ninth school year (age fifteen–sixteen). Growing up within a religiously active family, she decided to "take a closer look" at a religious vocation while in *Gymnasium.* Thus, in her *Oberstufe* studies in *Gymnasium* she concentrated on Protestant theology, English, and Latin, making those choices on her own without pressure from her family. She studied hard in preparation for the *Abitur* to satisfy her own ambitions and her father's high expectations of her. Although Anja's closest friends chose other universities, she chose Rhineland for study in theology, partly because her parents had attended Rhineland and partly because she wanted to develop new relationships. However, before she could enroll in the university as a theology major, Anja had to complete a six-month, full-time course in Greek and pass a demanding examination. Thus, when she began her theology studies, she was competent in both Greek and Latin in preparation for reading and research in her discipline.

Midwestern University

Mike was in his sixth semester as a religious studies major at Midwestern when he participated in his case study in an upper-level religion course in the spring semester of 2001. Mike was from a small town in Iowa and graduated from a small public high school in the area. He lived at home with his mother while attending university and was a nontraditional student in that he did not follow a straight path from high school to university. He began thinking about a call to Christian ministry while still in high school and started his postsecondary studies at a local Lutheran college where he took some general courses and a few religion courses. Since he had not formulated a clear direction for his life when he completed his fourth semester of study, Mike stopped his education and went to England for a year. When he returned to the United States, he began working as recreation director and tutor in a halfway house for people leaving prison on parole. He then began taking classes part-time while working as a staff member at the YMCA. He restarted his full-time education by entering Midwestern in the fall of 2000. It was then that he fully began religious studies and made a commitment to preparing for seminary.

The Students in Political Science

Rhineland University

Jana was in her first semester as a major in political science and history when she participated in her case study in the "tutorial" (seminar) portion of a large introductory political science course in the spring/summer semester of 1998. Jana was from a small town in North Rhine–Westphalia. Her family roots are there; her father was in machinery sales, while her mother was a shop assistant. Unlike the other German students in these case studies, Jana attended *Realschule* rather than *Gymnasium*. The difference is significant in terms of the overall pattern of Jana's education. Like Mike at Midwestern, she was a nontraditional student in the sense that she had worked full-time before deciding to qualify for university. While *Gymnasium* prepares students for university, *Realschule* prepares them for various commercial and technical vocations that in Germany are not perceived to require an academic background. Jana worked as a librarian's assistant for a couple of years, then decided that she did indeed want to go to university. She began attending a *Kolleg,* a school offering studies preparing students for the *Abitur*—the gateway to university. In her study for the *Abitur,* she concentrated on history and Latin. She then spent a year in Ireland as an au pair while studying English intensively. During this time she became interested in political matters as well as history and decided to major in both.

Midwestern University

Kevin was in his third semester at Midwestern but only his second semester as a political science major when he participated in his case study in a middle-level political science course in the fall of 2000. He had completed the required introductory courses in political science the previous semester. The course was open to a range of students, from sophomores to seniors. Kevin grew up in a small city in Illinois and graduated from his local high school. His father is a pharmacist and his mother had gone back to college for a degree after working in a public service capacity. He had several brothers and sisters still in the public schools. In high school, in addition to the general graduation requirements, Kevin took AP courses in American history and rhetoric, which like other courses in his school depended mostly on multiple-choice tests rather than extended writing. Like Jill and Sarah, Kevin also wrote for the school newspaper, mainly about sports, and most of his high school writing came from this activity. At the time of his case study participation, he had taken two political science courses at the introductory level.

The Students in English/Journalism
Rhineland University

Peter was in his ninth semester as a combined major in English and journalism when he participated in his case study in an upper-level course in the rhetoric of advertising in the fall of 1997. Peter grew up a small town in North Rhine–Westphalia and completed his *Abitur* at the local *Gymnasium.* His father worked for a chemical company. Peter was self-supporting, with a daughter whom he was helping to raise, and he planned his academic work partly around the schedule of care for her. In addition to the usual government benefits in travel passes and food for students, Peter received *Kindergeld,* a small government allotment to help with child care. In addition, he worked part-time for a moving company to help support himself and his daughter. In *Gymnasium,* Peter concentrated on social sciences, German, and math. He chose advertising as a major in hopes of getting a job in the advertising industry once he finished his degree. At Rhineland, journalism courses are part of the English department and focus strongly on rhetorical study. Peter had completed most of his course work and was preparing for his final examinations and eventually for a thesis.

Midwestern University

Toni was in her seventh semester as a double major in English and journalism when she took an upper-level course in modern poetry in the fall of 2000. Toni grew up with her mother and brother in a Phoenix suburb and attended high school there. Her mother was an administrative assistant and had completed a two-year college degree. As an African American student, Toni was in a small minority in her city and school, which had a sizable Hispanic minority but a small African American population. In addition to the general high school graduation requirements, Toni took several more English courses, including a year-long Advanced Placement course in English literature. Like Jill in history, Toni chose to take the national examinations in this AP course, so she wrote short analytic papers and practice examinations often in high school. She scored well on the exams and received college credit for them. Like all the other American students in this study, Toni wrote for her school newspaper, mainly feature articles and pieces about public service events. This experience encouraged her to choose English and journalism at university.

Appendix 2.1: Questions for Students' Writing History Interviews

1. What courses in high school required writing? What types of writing were required?

2. How did you learn to write these kinds of writing in high school?

3. In high school, where and when did you write?

4. What kinds of writing did you do outside the classroom?

5. How did you feel about yourself as a writer in high school?

6. What kinds of writing did you do in your first courses at university?

7. In what ways did the writing you did in high school prepare you for writing in the university?

8. In what ways were your high school writing experiences most helpful when you came to university?

9. In what ways were your high school writing experiences least helpful when you came to university?

10. What kinds of writing were you best prepared for when you came to university? least prepared for?

11. What kinds of writing are you required to do in your major courses?

12. How well were you prepared for the writing in your major courses when you first began taking them?

13. What kinds of courses do you take at the [lower, upper] level in your major? What kinds of writing do you do in these courses?

14. What expectations do your teachers have for your writing in these courses?

15. How do you go about developing a topic for the writing in these courses?

16. a. Could you describe the processes you use to plan, research, and write a term paper or other significant writing task?

    b. How do you position your own perspectives in relation to other viewpoints and interpretations?

    c. How do you articulate your own voice in connection with the voices of others you are reading and responding to?

17. What parts of your writing planning, preparation, composing, and revising do you do individually? with others, in class or outside of class? with the teacher?

18. In what ways is the term paper or other significant papers challenging or difficult, as compared to other kinds of writing in your major courses?

19. What kind(s) of readers do you envision when you write? Do you envision different kinds of readers for different kinds of writing?

20. How have your attitudes about yourself as a writer changed since you came to the university?

Appendix 2.2: Questions for Planning/Topic Formation Interview

1. Please describe this writing task as you now understand it. What is the purpose of the task or assignment?

2. Please describe the specific topic you are dealing with. What do you see as the relationship between this topic and the issues and subject matter of the course?

3. Describe the process by which you have developed the topic you plan to write about. What roles have your instructor and/or fellow students played in your topic development?

4. Describe how you will go about developing this writing task from this point. Specifically,

   • how will you organize your research and reading?

   • how will you use source readings in your project?

   • how will you select sources to read? from course materials, library reserve readings, open stack searches, Internet searches?

   • how will you develop your text—i.e., will you use outlines, personal rough drafts, or workshop drafts as text development steps?

6. Please describe the structure of your paper as you now envision it.

7. As you begin writing, to what extent will you respond to the views expressed in the written sources you have read? How important do you think the views of your teacher or other students will be to your writing?

8. What problems do you think you will encounter as you continue planning and writing this paper? How do you anticipate you might deal with them?

9. What readers do you envision as you plan and write this paper? How do you expect your awareness of your readers to shape your writing?

Appendix 2.3: Final Interview

1. How did the writing go? (Please give any answer or response you like.)

2. Please describe any collaborative work you did with other students for this writing project. If you did a group report,

   a. how did you share the work?

   b. how often did you meet? What did you talk about or do when you met together?

   c. did you produce a group text? How did you do this?

   d. did one person write the text, or did your collaborators write the text together as a group?

   If you worked in writing groups,

   a. how often you meet with your group?

   b. what draft stages did you share with your group?

   c. what kind of feedback did you receive from your group, and how was it communicated to you?

   d. what impact did group feedback have on your planning and writing activities?

3. What parts of your report did you use later in your seminar paper? How important was this report to your paper?

4. What did you learn during the semester from other students' reports and discussions in class? How did you use these reports and discussions in your own writing?

5. Could you describe the role that your instructor played in helping you develop your topic and write your paper?

6. Before you started this paper, how much did you know

about researching and writing such a paper? How much experience did you have in doing research? What experience did you have in planning and organizing a term paper?

7. When you wrote this paper, did you follow a process that you had already learned from your past experiences in writing? If so, could you describe that process?

8. What strategies, which you did not use earlier, did you have to develop to write this paper?

9. Did you have any problems in researching, planning, or writing this paper? How did you deal with them?

10. What did you learn from writing this paper?

11. How has the writing of this paper affected your view of yourself as a student in your major discipline?

12. How has the writing of this paper affected your view of yourself as a writer?

Appendix 2.4: Interview Questions for High School Teachers

1. In your opinion, what are the connections between learning and writing?

2. What kinds of writing do you think are most important for your students to learn in high school?

3. What purposes are served, in your view, by the writing students do in high school?

4. What writing activities do you emphasize in your teaching?

5. How much writing do students do at home and how much at school?

6. How do students develop topics for their writing? Do you give them topics? Do they develop their own topics?

7. How do you respond to students' writing?

8. How important for you are school, district, or state guidelines about writing?

9. In what ways do your teaching practices differ from the official guidelines about writing activities?

10. How much freedom do your students have in writing their texts? To what extent do you specify their topics or their papers?

11. In your opinion, what are the connections between writing in high school and writing at college/university?

12. In your opinion, what should be the most important outcomes of high school education for students as writers?

Appendix 2.5: Interview Questions for University Instructors

1. In your opinion, what are the connections between learning and writing?

2. What kinds of writing do you expect your students to have learned in high school? What writing abilities and preparations do you expect them to bring to university?

3. In your experience, what difficulties in writing do students have when they make the transition from high school to university?

4. What kinds of writing do you think are important for your students to learn in the early semesters of their study at university?

5. What are your expectations for students' writing in your discipline? What goals and practices do you expect students to develop as writers in your discipline?

6. In what ways does your department or program help students learn the goals and strategies needed for writing success in your discipline?

7. What writing abilities, skills, and activities do you emphasize in your courses? Why? On what writing abilities and skills do your courses concentrate?

8. In what ways do you seek to change or develop your students' writing abilities in your courses?

9. How do you respond to your students' writing? What are your goals in responding to students' writing, and what strategies do you use to achieve these goals?

10. What masteries do you expect of students as writers who have completed degrees in your discipline?

Note

1. A small percent of students earn an *Abitur* in *Gesamtschule* (comprehensive school), offered in some states as an alternative to the multiple pathways system. Another small percentage earn an *Abitur* later, after completing a nonacademic track and working, then re-enrolling in an academic preparation track.

3 / The Work of Writing: Student Authorship Roles in Cross-National Perspective

Timelines, Deadlines, Free Time: Time and Authorship Roles

Time is embedded in our daily routines in ways often too familiar to notice. Yet time structures reveal themselves in academic settings in various guises: as work schedules, project and paper deadlines, and exam schedules; as program time limits and financial pressures; and—perhaps most complex and variable—in academic writers' individual working rhythms for planning, researching, writing, and revising their texts. Identifying the impact of time structures on students' development as novice writers is not an easy task. Eviatar Zerubavel suggests that "normalcy" itself is a "temporally situated" construct full of "hidden rhythms" embedded in institutional and personal routines (20). Time patterns are difficult to discern, since they can readily seem transparent and part of the given in a learning environment. Such an effort requires a fresh look at material contexts that influence novice writers as they learn to participate in academic knowledge communities.

The power of time in the shaping of social practice is given major emphasis in the work of Anthony Giddens, who says that "the 'situatedness' of interaction in time and space . . . is at the very heart of social theory" (*Constitution* 110). He maintains that "the time-space paths that the members of a community or society follow in their day-to-day activities" are "strongly influenced by, and also reproduce, basic institutional parameters of the social systems in which they are implicated" (142–43). Giddens's analysis suggests that novice participants in communities of practice must identify and internalize their temporal patterns as they learn to participate.

The importance of temporal patterns in students' work as writers has been particularly noted by researchers in the genre studies tradition. Studies by Patricia Dunmire, John M. Swales, and Elaine Chin have illuminated aspects of time and space in specific knowledge communities. Chin, studying the activities of journalism students, shows how institutional expectations are conveyed through material structures and interpreted by students as motives for writing. In another study, Swales explores time patterns embedded in different knowledge communities located in a single university building, noting a pattern of "different floors, different clocks," as each community's activities are shaped by "separate, highly temporal rhythms" governing their practices (30). In these studies, temporal patterns emerge as crucial elements of the roles students develop as writers in active knowledge communities.

Institutional Time Structures

It is the tradition of free-time writing that most differentiates German students' roles as writers from those of American students. The differing time structures in the American and German learning environments are clearly implicated in students' practices as writers. The semester durations of the two universities in this study are similar. Rhineland University has two semesters of roughly fifteen weeks, one beginning in October and ending in February, the other beginning in April and ending in July. Midwestern follows the American pattern of fifteen-week fall and spring semesters. German and American students both enjoy an approximately three-month summer break, though the American students get only one month off for winter break while the German students get about two. There is a striking contrast, however, in the zoning of institutional time in relation to students' practices as writers, reflecting different expectations about students' roles as writers in their disciplines.

Deadlines, Free Time, and Autonomy

All "social formations" have "their own temporal styles of life" (187), says Christopher Gosden. In the context of a particular formation, "time and action become synonymous" so that the temporal styles of institutions, for example, are instantiated in the habits and practices of participants (192). The American postsecondary educational system is based on a temporally organized regulatory structure, which measures students in part by their ability to plan and write texts against persistent in-semester and semester-end deadlines. This productivity is segmented and timed by the evaluative processes embedded in the credit/grade point–reporting system shared by most American colleges and universities. Undergraduate courses at Midwestern reflect this pattern. Since courses meet two or three times per week, students are evaluated at frequent intervals by quizzes, tests, short papers, and group and individual reports, which come much more frequently than for German students. End-of-semester deadlines drive completion of semester papers and projects. Because of the expectations and pressure of semester credit/grade point calculations, unfinished work from undergraduates is not easily tolerated. Correspondingly, the periods between semesters are generally unregulated by any institutional expectations, aside from voluntary additional work such as summer school course work, between-semester projects, or field trips.

At Rhineland University, time patterns and institutional expectations for student productivity are different. Courses meet typically once a week, and student tasks are more widely spaced. As in most German universities, Rhineland University students do not face institutionally enforced semester-by-semester credit/grade point evaluation. The university does not insist that students complete courses they begin; they are free to come to lectures and discussions without doing credit work. Rhineland University students in this study—and German students generally—are largely free to pursue degrees at their own rate of study. Few universities enforce official time frames suggested for degree completion, so students are typically free to take as many semesters as they wish or have financial means for.

The issue of graduation time pressure marks a crucial difference between German and American national attitudes about postsecondary education. In the German system, students' autonomy in making individual course writing choices signifies a systemic tolerance for students' variable learning time frames. Indeed, the latitude permitted by this tradition of individual choice has become a vexed issue in German educational politics. German students take much longer to finish their first degrees than the governments and universities would like, in view of the rising costs of education. According to recent figures, German students spend a national average of one to three years more than American students in completing their first degrees, though completion times vary among disciplines. For example, history majors in German universities take an average of twelve to fourteen semesters to complete their first degrees (a master's or a *Diplom*), political science majors eleven to thirteen semesters, and religious studies majors ten to twelve semesters (Statistisches Bundesamt). In contrast, nearly 80 percent of American undergraduates earning baccalaureate degrees in private institutions and about 50 percent of those in public institutions finish in eight semesters (National Association 24). As a result, there have been many calls in Germany for tightening up time requirements for degree completion, but the pattern is still widespread in the German system.

The most distinctive time structure inscribed in Rhineland University students' authorship roles is the practice of free-time writing/revising. As I have indicated elsewhere (Foster and Russell), this practice is a major feature of German students' autonomy as learner/writers. In German universities, students must learn to be responsible for establishing their own deadlines in becoming productive writers, as opposed to American students' obligation to meet the point-to-point, on-time writing productivity goals demanded by the American credit/grade point system. The German students in this study were given wide latitude by most professors in choosing when and where to write seminar papers. Most faculty were willing to accept completed seminar papers whenever students finished them—at semester's end, later during semester break, even after the next semester began. The students typically wrote papers in the time between semesters—either in the February-to-April period between winter and summer semesters or in the July-to-October period between summer and winter semesters.

Free-time writing/revising is a basic practice of Rhineland University's students. The sanction for this practice is inscribed in the university's semester calendar, which is officially divided into two parts, the "lecture time" and the "lecture-free time" (*vorlesungsfreie*

Zeit). (The dates in the following list correspond to the periods of case studies at each university.)

INSTITUTIONAL CALENDARS

Midwestern University

August 23, 1999	fall semester begins
December 17, 1999	fall semester ends
January 18, 2000	spring semester begins
May 14, 2000	spring semester ends

Rhineland University

October 1, 1997	winter semester begins
October 15, 1997	winter semester classes begin (lecture time starts)
February 10, 1998	winter semester classes end (lecture-free time starts)
March 31, 1998	winter semester ends
April 1, 1998	summer semester begins
April 15, 1998	summer semester classes begin (lecture time starts)
July 15, 1998	summer semester classes end (lecture-free time starts)
September 30, 1998	summer semester ends

The lecture time at Rhineland University is the period when classes (lectures and seminars) are in session, what Americans would call the actual academic semester—at Rhineland University roughly the same as at Midwestern, about three and a half months. It includes class meetings and a week or so of exams afterward. The officially labeled lecture-free time is all the time when classes are not in session, from the end of exams of one semester until the official beginning of the next semester. This official designation identifies between-semester periods as academically regulated time and invites students to construe this time as academic work time (though of course students may also work at jobs or travel in this time). It invites them to see themselves as active knowledge-community participants throughout the calendar year. The more power an individual has over professional time boundaries, the higher the status, argues Zerubavel: "Flexibly defined temporal boundaries of professional commitments are usually associated with high status, rigidly defined ones with low status" (152). German students' freedom to complete projects in the lecture-free time between semesters gives them the authority to control the boundaries of work and private time and confers the autonomy characteristic of experienced participants in knowledge fields.

It was during the lecture-free time that most German students in this study wrote their seminar papers. Vera, a combined history and English major whose seminar project is described below, noted that most instructors "don't give you a certain date, like on 31 March it is due. They say just 'finish it.'" Peter, an English/journalism major, described his perception of the postsemester period as an integral part of university work:

> Normally we do [writing] after the time the courses take place, so we have about two months to finish the paper. We normally have to hand them in by the actual end of the term, which is the end of September or the end of March. I don't think of this time as vacation. As long as I have to write a paper, it's not a vacation. . . . I think it belongs to the semester.

Peter's attitude is shared by the other German students in this study. For them, free-time planning/writing is a component of their work as academic writers. Unlike American students, they do not segment their academic work into "school time" and "vacation" but instead view writing as an ongoing activity throughout the year. As the authorship practices of the German students described below show, a self-directed, reflexive autonomy emerges as an important element in their development as learner/writers.

Case Study Comparisons and Time and Task Patterns

To illustrate these time-pattern comparisons, I describe the work of two pairs of students in detail—upper-level history majors and upper-level religious studies majors. The first pair consists of Vera (seventh-semester history at Rhineland University) in an upper-level history seminar and Jill (eighth-semester history major at Midwestern University) in a senior seminar in history. The second pair consists of Anja (sixth-semester religious studies major at Rhineland University) in an upper-level religion seminar and Mike (a sixth-semester religious studies major at Midwestern University) in an upper-level religion course. (See tables 3.1 and 3.2.) Other case study students will be mentioned in the discussion that follows, though they will not receive detailed description. These include lower-level history majors Kirsten (German) and Sarah (American), political science majors Jana (German) and Kevin (American), and English/journalism majors Peter (German) and Toni (American).

German: Vera's Upper-Level Seminar in History

Vera's total task period:	October 1–January 28
Total task duration:	sixteen weeks
Text outcome:	one 8,000-word paper

Vera, studying to become a history teacher at the secondary level, was a full-time student and did not work outside her academic obligations. She had already taken several upper-level seminars in history (and English, another major) when she began the upper-level seminar entitled Foreign Economics, Political Regimes, and Development Strategies in Latin America, 1920–1980, taught by a specialist in economic history and meeting once a week for two hours. There were about twenty-five students in the class, most in their third or fourth year of study. The instructor's strong expectations for students' capabilities led him to formulate a complex set of individual and group tasks in the course. He placed students' group work at the center of each course meeting so that students had both group responsibilities for classroom activities and individual responsibility for researching and writing their seminar papers. Students were asked to choose one of two roles as an "expert"—as a country specialist or as a topic specialist—and to base their classroom activities and their seminar paper topics on their areas of expertise. The instructor noted that he divided the thirty students in the course into related "country" and "thematic [topic-related]" groups responsible for managing the two-hour meetings: "The thematic group has to prepare a discussion for each meeting, and the country groups are to [organize] the [country-specific] material to fit the thematical group's topic." Thus, students' group activities were the main focus of course meetings throughout the regular semester, each entailing a handout bibliography and prepared presentation/discussions.

The instructor intended the students' classroom activities to broaden their understanding of Latin American economic issues and problems and to help them define and develop seminar paper projects. "What people should learn from this," he said, "is to find out rapidly what are the important questions and issues . . . [and] how to find various materials to answer these questions":

> As members of country groups they are to find various materials to answer these questions. And [in their classroom presentations] they are to present a country case study. . . . So writing a case study is something I want to teach them. And when I go through the plan of the papers [in individual conferences], this is where the teaching of writing case studies [comes in].

Since these were third- and fourth-year students, the instructor expected them to know strategies for planning and writing seminar papers:

> In a *Hauptseminar,* you expect them to know how writing happens and how to find literature for their theme for the [paper] . . . to follow a certain logic and line of argument, to formulate the argument and develop the text that develops the argument in an intelligible way.

The instructor also expected students to know how to incorporate sources of information and different critical viewpoints "to know how [this literature] may bear on their argument, how to place them in a text, how to produce a text." Vera's case shows how important this enabling knowledge was to her successful completion of the seminar project.

CHRONOLOGY OF TASK ACTIVITIES

First week October	Began semester course meetings—"lecture time." First meeting with teacher to discuss topic.
Second week October	Began collecting sources from public and central university libraries.
Fourth week October	Second meeting with teacher for source advice. Collected sources from Latin American Studies department.
November–early December	Read source material; developed topic issues.
First week December	Third meeting with teacher to review source list and revise plan for paper.
Second week December	Began writing/revising second week of December. Continued during Christmas holiday and through January.
Last week January	Completed and submitted paper.

Phase One: Topic inquiry
Week 1: October 6–11

Since the instructor had asked students to try to complete papers within a week of the close of lecture time of the winter semester (February), Vera met with her professor about her country choice and paper topic as soon as the course started. Wanting to maintain as long a planning timeline as possible and realizing that she would need an extended resource search (given her basic lack of knowledge about Cuba and

Latin America generally), she began forming her topic quickly within the first weeks of class. From hard experience in her early seminars, she had learned that she worked best when she had ongoing direction from instructors as she formed and researched her topic. As a result, she quickly began building a relationship with her instructor, a professor with a distinguished research record, in this course. She visited him in the first week of classes to choose Cuba as her country of interest, and the instructor suggested she focus on the tensions between "populism and socialism in the days of the early Cuban revolution." Deciding that she needed a quick overview of Cuban history before going any further, she went immediately to the city library and got two popular books about Cuba to give her a general understanding of its postrevolutionary period. She was excited by her teacher's challenge to become an "expert" in a specific area, and she sensed that he was willing to work more closely with her than most other instructors had. "I mean, he did more than you have to do as a professor. And when you go to the *Sprechstunde* [office hour], you feel that he is really interested in helping you, not like, you know, 'Hurry up; go.'" Finding her instructor willing to meet with her whenever she wished, she began to rely on his advice in developing a clear focus and finding useful sources, always the most difficult task in writing a seminar paper.

The next week she went back to his office to negotiate her paper topic:

> I asked him whether I could write about the topic area he had suggested. He replied that it was just meant as a sort of guideline . . . and if I were interested I might want to write about the workers and the union movement after the revolution. I told him what I would like to do, that I wanted to write on Cuba, on workers maybe. We worked it out together then that I could work on the Cuban workers and unions after the revolution until 1973.

Vera liked this topic, since it gave a human face to the socialist tensions she was interested in, so she began identifying research sources and planning her paper immediately.

Her previous experience in seminar project development helped her recognize that, given her lack of knowledge of the area, she faced a difficult planning and resource-gathering process. She then began searching for scholarly sources:

> The first and basic problem was that I didn't know anything about Cuba at all except for Fidel Castro. And there was the problem that there's hardly any literature on the Cuban working class in the Rhineland University history department.

Her teacher actively mentored Vera's search for sources on Cuban labor issues. He told Vera early on that "it wouldn't be easy to find enough literature about my topic at [Rhineland University]" and suggested some libraries in other universities within a train ride of Rhineland. As a result, "I went to [a nearby university] and the sociology department [at Rhineland University] and looked on the Internet." From these broad searches she found a variety of books and articles as well as a reliable Internet database, which her instructor had helped her track down.

Phase Two: Text planning/research
Weeks 2–9: October 13–December 12

Vera began searching for scholarly sources just after meeting with her professor. By early December, she had gathered about a dozen books and documents from six different resource sites, copied books and articles, highlighted relevant passages, and written detailed note cards. As a prewriting strategy, she organized her topic into main sections and key words and constructed a section-by-section plan for her paper, then went for the third time to her instructor to ask his advice on the plan. He was glad to respond, because as he noted, he liked to go over students' plans with them: "I go through [their plans] and ask what do you write here, and you should be able to explain why you organize it this way." Reviewing the plan with her, he suggested that she expand the section on labor laws affecting workers' lives and her section on workers' class consciousness. She was grateful for his extensive help:

With the [planning outline] he was very good, too, because I wouldn't have thought about this, to write about the laws. And he gave me important direction when he talked about the table of contents. He took much effort to explain to me what he thought about this and this. This was quite good. Not every professor does this.

Phase Three: Composing/revising
Weeks 10–16: December 12–January 28

After her third conference with her instructor, Vera began drafting her paper. Throughout December and into January, as her daily schedule of other course work allowed, she methodically wrote sections while rereading sources and continuing to look for new ones:

> I began writing in the middle of December after I had read all my sources. But I kept an eye open for further sources while I had already started writing. I prepared one [section] on one day and typed it into the computer the next day. . . . I revised a bit . . . when I saw that something didn't fit with what I wrote on another page. Most of the revisions I did in the introduction part and in the last part.

She surrounded herself with her notes and sources: "I arrange my notes . . . in the order I want to use them. . . . I make a list of notes, items I want to use in the text." Her notes are both direct source quotes—"what I think is important myself"—and interpretations and commentary in her own words, as "I find my own thoughts and add them. And then I start typing it at the computer."

The most difficult section for Vera was the final section in which she drew some conclusions about the changing role of workers' class consciousness in the evolution of postrevolutionary Cuba: "I changed this three or four times," she said, "because it's hard to make a conclusion out of twenty pages." When she had finished a draft of the entire paper, she went over it again for a final review: "I did a general revision after I had finished writing the whole paper." It was at this point late in January that Vera's "country group" had been scheduled for their classroom presentation/discussion (the last course meeting of the semester). From this interaction, Vera made some changes to the introduction and conclusion. In the days following, she gave the completed draft to her mother and to a friend for their feedback, then "having done the revisions I printed out the paper again and sent it to another friend to tell me her opinion. I made the last changes on [the day it was handed in]." The result of this deliberate, extended writing activity was a paper of about 8,000 words and twenty-four pages entitled "The Worker and Labor Union Movement of Cuba." It received a grade of 3+ (approximately a C+), and the instructor made many marginal notations about syntax, orthography, and citation form, along with a few comments about issues being discussed. While the instructor found it "well-written" and "interesting" in its main points, he also found it deficient in the use of formal conventions of source use. Brief end comments included "comprehensively framed . . . interesting viewpoint . . . formal issues: many errors in sentences and bibliography." The instructor's frequent marginal markings suggest that Vera's paper did not meet his standards of writing usage or citation form. Vera accepted his judgment equably, noting that all her professors had criticized the mechanics and style of her writing. She felt good about the quality and clarity of her arguments, which gave her confidence that she could continue to write successfully as she completed her degree: "I felt quite assured that I got a 3+ because I had quite a good feeling with this. I knew that it wouldn't be a 1 [an A] because I never write 1s. So I mean I have the feeling that I can manage my university study, I hope."

American: Jill's Senior Seminar in History

Jill's total task period:	March 10–April 7
Total task duration:	four weeks
Text outcome:	one 4,000-word paper

Jill was enrolled in a senior seminar in modern European history with about a dozen students in her last semester. During this period,

Jill faced both academic and private time pressures. In addition to a standard load of course work (fifteen semester hours), she was working nearly full-time as the manager of a coffee shop. The temporal boundaries of her study, writing, and work overlapped frequently so that she was often reading and planning her writing in the cramped confines of her back office amid the aromas of latte and cappuccino. Though she was a senior in her final semester and had already taken a dozen courses in history, this was Jill's first seminar (only one was required for the history major). Her seminar was similar to a German seminar, focusing on the students' research/writing projects and featuring students' presentations and discussions as the primary classroom activities. However, for her the seminar tasks—two research-based writing projects requiring extensive resource searches—were of greater magnitude than what she had faced before as a history major. In previous history courses, she had written short papers (three to five pages) focusing on specific course-related issues and had written many essay examinations for which, she said, "you could still use the generic formula of the five-paragraph essay to get your point across." And she had written term papers—the biography of an African leader in one course, a term paper on an American president's legacy in another—that were extensions of course discussions and required some library research. But the seminar writing tasks required a combination of extensive source research and complex historical arguments that went beyond her previous experiences.

Moreover, unlike a German seminar with one long-term, cumulative project, Jill's seminar required two semester papers of about fifteen pages each on completely different topics, one due about five weeks into the semester and one during the last month of the semester. As a result, Jill's work was segmented into two successive, unrelated research/writing projects with only a month available for the first one. For this chapter's purposes, her first, shorter project is described here briefly, followed by a fuller analysis of the second project, which shows her most fully developed research/writing practices as an undergraduate history major.

To begin her first seminar paper, she met briefly with her instructor in late January to construct her topic, a study of the German

Social-Democratic Party before and during World War I. He communicated to her his expectations that students would develop their own independent analyses of historical events by looking carefully at primary sources. Indeed, he believed that helping students "learn how to get to the primary sources" was a difficult but essential challenge for teachers. He wanted to help students understand that "it's not just giving an opinion off the top of your head, but an opinion that is rooted in the historical event. . . . You can't just shoot off an emotional reaction to something. You've got to be able to document it."

Jill gathered several books about a week before her paper was due in mid-February, read as much as she could, and—following the pattern of short-burst writing that had enabled her to succeed as an academic up to now—outlined and wrote the paper in two days. In retrospect, she was not happy with the process or the outcome. Once she had gotten into it, the topic had proved more complex than she had anticipated. She concluded that time pressure had driven her to write the paper before she had adequately addressed the scope of the task: "I chose a topic," she says,

> that was fairly complicated, and you know, in the time and space I had to work with it, it was difficult to come to a very good understanding of what my topic was. . . . My research was, I don't want to use the word "shallow," but basically that's what it is. I couldn't read enough, know enough to present it successfully. The sources required a lot more attention than I could give them.

When she got her paper back in early March with the instructor's comments, Jill saw that her haste in trying to incorporate multiple sources resulted in many citation and contextualizing lapses that were strongly noted in "a lot of red marking in my paper. . . . [The instructor] wrote 'failing to introduce a quote . . . [or] to give background.'" Jill decided that because her instructor valued students' clear analyses in relation to primary sources and because paper deadlines and work obligations exerted constant pressure, her next paper topic would have to be based on fewer, more easily accessible primary sources.

Jill's experience with this critique does suggest the advantage of the American pattern of ongoing feedback from multiple writing assignments within a semester. Her instructor made clear that he liked the seminar setting specifically because it enabled him to give clear feedback to students about their writing:

> Within the seminar context, we have one-on-one meetings. I'll mention, "Well, look at what you did on this first time around that you've got to keep an eye for this or this or this." I'm conscious of the problems and weakness of each student, and I think they're under very significant pressure to improve, because they know that I know their writing problems.

With her instructor's comments on her mind, Jill began thinking about her second seminar paper.

CHRONOLOGY OF TASK ACTIVITIES

First week March	Met with teacher, set topic.
Last week March	Began collecting sources from university library (after spring break, during which she did no academic work).
First week April	Began reading, assimilating sources.
April 7, 10 AM	Began writing paper.
April 7, 7 PM	Submitted paper in seminar.

Phase One: Topic inquiry
March 7: Conference with instructor

The schedule set by the instructor dictated that the completed second paper was due on April 7, and Jill decided in the March 7 conference with her professor to limit the scope of it: "The second paper I chose was more narrow than the first . . . as far as time frame was concerned, as well as the kind of topic it was." The topic she chose was Germany's legislative treatment of the Jews from 1933 to 1939, which enabled her to rely on easily obtained *New York Times* articles as primary sources as well as books readily available in the library. With this topic, "it was a lot easier to find the sources that I needed." Jill described her subject:

> The second paper was supposed to be on post–World War I, so my general interest was in the concentration camps of Nazi Germany. [The instructor] directed me towards the beginning of the anti-Semitic movement in Nazi Germany. So basically my topic, as it came out of our discussion, was a treatment of the Jews from 1933 to 1939, from Hitler's initial coming to power, and then before the ghetto, the camps in Poland. So that was a narrow enough topic that it was manageable.

Believing that she could locate primary sources for this topic easily, Jill left the conference hopeful that she could plan and write her paper quickly after spring break ended. During the break, Jill spent most of her time working in the coffee shop and did no planning or research during the rest of March.

Phase Two: Text planning/research
April 1–6

In an intense week of effort after spring break ended, between April 1 and April 6, Jill located, organized, and scanned her sources. In this final month of the spring semester, ready source acquisition and manageability were primary considerations. As the semester moved to its final weeks, she was managing several term paper projects in other courses: "I learned how to work faster from the first paper, which is still not very fast. . . . In truth, I didn't have the time. You know. I was split up between other things." Luckily for her, she found that the "*New York Times* covered these events very closely. And, you know, in a way you take a risk by hoping that it covers that and I lucked out." One anthology of German anti-Semitic laws and the *New York Times* news stories served as her most significant primary sources.

> This [anthology] included letters and things like that, that Hitler had written long before he even wrote *Mein Kampf.*

. . . Those kind of clue you in to make [your] understanding more complete and give you those clues that make the picture more colorful.

At first she took the time to use the notation system she had developed from earlier research tasks, writing key words and quotes on "junior legal pads." But she knew she had to work more quickly to assimilate the key primary sources she intended to rely on. She laid out her materials on various surfaces in her room, and "it was with those books and the copies of the *New York Times* articles that I sat down to write my paper."

Phase Three: Composing/revising
April 7

Jill's paper was due at 7 PM on April 7, when her seminar met; she began writing at 10 AM that day. She relied on the high-intensity, short-burst writing strategy she had practiced with success in her four years of university study. She preferred to write a paper all at once to keep her train of thought: "In order to write the paper, I don't want to have an idea at one point and not be able to remember it by the time I sit down the second time to write it." With her books and notes around her, she began

with an outline, like a rough outline, I just sketch it down on a piece of paper before I sit down at the computer to write. I had the picture of the paper in my mind . . . what order [the issues] would be in, and how they'd overlap. That doesn't come until I sit down and write.

She organized her materials in piles that signified major issues:

All the books I set up right in front of me on my desk. . . .
Nazi mentality [sources] were in this pile; all law sources were in this pile; personal narrative in another pile. I just stack the books up that way. It's kind of an organized mess, I'd say.

Within this thematically arranged physical space, Jill began writing. The result of this intensive writing was a paper of 4,000 words and fourteen pages, delivered on time in the evening seminar.

The instructor gave the paper a B+ but made no general comment summarizing his response. Rather, there were marginal notes asking for elaboration of some factual statements and generalizations at some points in the text. There were few comments on her source usage and citations, suggesting that she had mastered the formal conventions of source use well enough to satisfy the instructor. She was thoughtful in retrospect about what the seminar projects meant to her as a learner/writer in history: "When [I] start to write, it makes you examine both yourself and the topic." She valued the reflexiveness that she found in her self-directed seminar projects and was regretful that she did not spend more time on the projects—"Time is the only thing that keeps me from [better writing]." At the same time, she enjoyed knowing that she could write fluently under time pressure: "I felt pretty good about it. I feel that I can produce good writing. I mean, I can say what I want to say and say it fluently and clearly. But I think I could be better."

Table 3.1 Upper-Level History Students

Text and Task Features	German Vera, 7th semester	American Jill, 8th semester
Task	seminar term paper	seminar term paper
Topic formation	1 week	3 weeks
Planning/research	8 weeks	6 days
Composing/revising	7 weeks	1 day
Total task duration	16 weeks	4 weeks
Paper length	8,000 words	4,000 words

German: Anja's Upper-Level Religion Seminar

Anja's total task period:	October 28–April 20
Total task duration:	twenty-three weeks
Text outcome:	one twenty-seven-page paper, 6,000 words

Anja was studying to become a religion teacher at the *Gymnasium* level. She had completed three upper-level religion seminars as well as several more seminars in pedagogy and English, her secondary concentrations. In this seminar for upper-level students entitled Questions of Authorship: John the Evangelist, the instructor, a senior scholar in New Testament theology, identified the seminar goal as helping students learn "the kind of work appropriate to constructing a particular topic" in the field of New Testament study. He expected only well-qualified students who had done "acceptable work" in earlier seminars to enroll in this course. The instructor wanted students to "investigate a particular topic" by means of "regular participation in the seminar [discussions]," which could lead, if they chose, to a paper. Thus Anja's seminar—with about twenty students—was centered on student work. The instructor assigned a biblical or interpretive passage as a discussion prompt to begin each weekly meeting; students were expected to sustain discussion in response. He offered no syllabus, no list of suggested topics, and only a brief reading list to supplement the biblical text. Nor was there any mention of a deadline for the paper. Instead, the course demanded students' self-starting, self-directed planning and writing to produce a seminar paper.

In the early course meetings, Anja came to feel that "it is bound to be an interesting seminar." She thought the discussions were challenging and occasionally "exhausting" as the class grappled with complex questions of theological interpretation in the book of John—issues of Christology and discipleship as well as legitimation, textuality, and authority. Anja found his "interest in our personal thoughts and ideas" exciting, believing that discussions of students' views were "more important than just reciting famous theologians like Bultmann or Becker." In class discussions, she discovered that the instructor "listens to all of our points and never qualifies a statement as inferior to another and never wants us to take over his opinions." To help students learn the perspectivist stance he believed necessary for biblical interpretation, the instructor "supplied us with a lot of different ways to understand and interpret the Gospel of St. John. There is no absolute truth that can be learned. One has to find his/her own way of understanding it." As the semester went along, she found herself "encouraged by our lively discussions" to begin "developing a theological identity" and to think carefully about the topic for her paper.

CHRONOLOGY OF TASK ACTIVITIES

Fourth week October	Lecture time. Began seminar participation.
Third week February through last week March	End of lecture time. Met with instructor to negotiate paper topic.
First week April	Planned and researched paper. Began drafting paper.
Third week April	Revised and submitted paper in second week of new semester.

Phase One: Topic formation
Weeks 1–15: October 28–February 15

Anja had spent the fifteen weeks of the regular semester reading widely in New Testament interpretation and participating in class discussions. In mid-February, at the end of the regular class meetings, she knew she had to pick a specific paper topic. She decided to focus on Jesus' "I am" words of John 14:6 ("I am the way, the truth, and the life") as a locus of many interpretive challenges in the book of John. Her instructor agreed and suggested a number of commentaries and studies. Though Anja had been "a bit nervous about how he would take to my ideas," she found him "helpful" and was invited to come back and "check with him whether I am on the right track." With this encouragement, she began assimilating her sources, which she had little trouble finding in the holdings of the university and departmental libraries, strong in the traditions of theological study. She began reading her sources and developing a detailed plan for her paper.

Phase Two: Topic planning/research
Weeks 16–20: February 23–April 1 (lecture-free time begins February 16)

From her conference with her instructor, Anja decided that her paper should include a textual exegesis of the primary text in its original

Greek (Anja had learned Greek to qualify for the upper level of theological study), followed by "comparisons of the commentaries" and concluded by her own interpretation in relation to them. She made several visits to both the university and the departmental libraries to gather more source material, working methodically through the earlier commentaries of Bauer and Bultmann to more recent works. Making copies of relevant sections of the commentaries, she took them home to read and underline in color-coded pens. She fashioned an extensive outline of her paper, including sections labeled "Text," "Analysis," and "Interpretation," the last part consisting of her own conclusions. She wanted to have a second conference with the instructor to get his feedback on her paper plan, but "he offered only one [office hour] during the whole *vorlesungsfreie Zeit* [free period between semesters], and I wasn't in [town] at this time so I couldn't go and see him." Instead she decided to go ahead and begin writing.

Phase Three: Composing/revising
Weeks 21–23: April 1–April 20

During this period, Anja began drafting the paper section by section. After composing the first section, she "decided to go see my mom about what I had written so far." She valued her mother's feedback because she was an experienced *Gymnasium* instructor of languages and theology with a strong background in Anja's subject matter. With her mother's comments carefully noted, Anja wrote a comparative analysis of the interpretive commentaries she had gathered, then identified "one meaning [as most convincing] and gave reasons for my decision." From this comparative background, she then began what she felt was the hardest part of her task, to "combine these different aspects and come up with a logical interpretation [of my own]." She did a linguistic analysis of the key words in the textual passage, analyzed their semantic contexts, and shaped her own interpretation from her analyses.

She then faced the task of positioning her own interpretation in relation to established views. She noted that she felt ready for this because of the semester-long discussions in class and the accumulated research she had done: "Now I had arrived at the stage which I thought would be the most interesting, the comparison of seven different interpretations of this verse." She was surprised and encouraged by what she found:

> It was surprising to me to find out that the commentators had not analyzed the verse as I had, not even one. But I think I have a strong point here and that is why I decided to stick with it. . . . I wrote down where I am of different opinion than the other theologians and then stated why.

During this period, Anja edited her paper, gave it to a friend to read for her reactions, and checked the citation conventions required in her discipline. On April 20 she submitted the paper, just after the beginning of the lecture time in the next semester.

To Anja's astonishment, her paper earned only a C+, despite what she felt was its presentation of a well-grounded context of scholarly views culminating in her own clearly stated conclusions. The instructor wrote that while she had analyzed the text well, "in my opinion the interpretation of John 14:6 is unfortunately mistaken." This judgment astounded Anja, who believed that she was being punished for making her personal interpretive claim so boldly. She had expected better of her paper, believing that she had supported her views with clear arguments responsive to established interpretations. Particularly because the instructor had encouraged the students to articulate their own ideas about interpretive issues, she was disappointed and angry about his reaction: "He always said in the seminar, 'Stick to your own thoughts and feelings and interpretations. Try to prove from the text that your feeling and interpretation is right.' That's what I did in the [paper], but apparently it wasn't THAT much right!" Anja's disappointment highlights a major disadvantage of free-time composing for German students: since instructors are not usually available in lecture-free times between semesters, she had no opportunity to get feedback on her emerging interpretation as she drafted and revised her paper. She said that she "would have liked to have had some sort of confirmation" that she was on the right track regarding her topic. Yet at the same time, Anja was able to see a positive side to this outcome: "I am really pleased with the result" because, she added, "I know I shouldn't say this, but this mark is really good for theology."

American: Mike's Upper-Level Religion Course

Mike's total task period:	January 16–May 14
Total task duration:	fifteen weeks
Text outcome:	one ten-page term paper, 3,450 words

Mike was enrolled in an upper-level religion course with fifteen students entitled Prophetic Literature of the Old Testament. He had taken a few religion courses previously at Midwestern and more—including studies in the New Testament—before that at another institution. Mike felt a call for the ministry and so regarded this course as an apprenticeship move toward seminary. In this regard, Mike was unique among the other students in the class, who represented a wide variety of majors and backgrounds. Most were not religious studies majors. Though designed as an upper-level offering in the official course schedule, this course—like most other upper-level humanities courses at Midwestern—enrolled students in their second through fourth years of study. The key was not their level of study but whether they had finished basic requirements. This diversity in students' semesters of study meant that while the instructor might anticipate some familiarity with the Bible, he could not assume students' familiarity with critical or analytical Bible study or much experience with extended writing tasks. Assigned readings included prophetic books of the Old Testament and two historical/interpretive studies of the prophets. Writing assignments included a short midterm paper, a classroom oral presentation on one prophetic text, and "a paper on the prophet presented in class . . . due at the end of the course." Hoping to get a better sense later of students' readiness for the critical study of biblical texts, the instructor made no specific statement of scope or length of this end-of-course paper in the syllabus or in the early weeks of the course.

Early in the semester, Mike chose the book of Amos as the prophetic text on which his class presentation and eventually his term paper would be based: "I wanted to get [the oral presentation] done and out of the way [so it would] correspond with the rest of my semester." Another factor was an ongoing relationship with his church pastor, who told him that "Amos was his favorite prophet and I wanted to find out why or what Amos had to say."

CHRONOLOGY OF TASK ACTIVITIES

Second week February	Gave oral presentation on book of Amos.
Second week April	Planned and wrote a short mid term paper.
Second week of May	Planned and wrote term paper.

Phase One: Topic formation
Weeks 1–7: January 16–February 27

During this period, Mike read assigned prophetic texts and participated in classroom discussions. Having chosen Amos as his long-term focus, he arranged an oral presentation in which he led a discussion of selected passages. He did not meet with the instructor during this period, confident that he could organize his class presentation on his own. He and his presentation partner decided to "do an activities book" to liven up the presentation, with a "reading of Amos incorporated into the activities." They devised a colored map of the ancient Near East to show "the way Amos . . . bounces back and forth, getting closer and closer to Israel." For the broad range of students in their course, they wanted to demonstrate in a lively way that Amos "was a herdsman and a tree dresser" and not "a professional prophet." To accompany the visual activities, Mike offered a "reading" of Amos based on two interpretive commentaries that were contained in the assigned course readings. In developing his reading, Mike felt "very much directed by these [commentary] authors. . . . I looked to them as like a guide" in this early interpretive effort. He noted after this presentation that he saw it as "almost like an early draft leading to the [final] paper," including references to the commentaries, but he did no actual planning for his term paper at this time.

Phase Two: Classroom participation/midterm paper
Weeks 8–16: February 18–May 7

During this period, Mike did nothing more with the book of Amos. He continued classroom discussions of various Old Testament prophets and wrote a five-page paper on a specific theme in the prophetic writings: "There's a messenger formula that [the instructor] taught us. And we're supposed to go through these prophets and . . . pick out the points of the messenger formula [and show how these points contain the] accusation, the sentence, and the actual messenger formula." Mike planned to spend "at least six hours, give or take an hour or so," in writing this paper. He also planned to include the views of two commentators whose texts were part of the assigned reading list of the course. While this topic generally covered the Old Testament prophets, it was not directly connected to Mike's projected term paper on Amos. In the later weeks of April, as the semester's end drew closer, the instructor urged (but did not require) students to meet with him to plan their final papers. However, Mike—procrastinating in a way he came to regret—did not use the opportunity to meet with the professor or to begin planning for the term paper.

Then one day in late April the term paper developed into a major flash point for Mike and other students in the prophets course. Many of them, including Mike, had assumed that it was to be "a five-page paper concerning the prophet researched for the class presentation . . . to demonstrate [an] understanding of that prophet and how [his book] fits the [tradition of the] prophetic books." But given the generality of the "major paper" phrase in the original syllabus, Mike and his fellow students grew concerned about just how many pages the instructor actually expected: "The syllabus is kind of hard to read for the [paper] assignment." As Mike told it, "A student said, 'Are you thinking along five pages or twenty pages?' and [the instructor] said, 'I'd lean more toward the twenty pages.' And that's when I realized I needed to put a little more effort into this paper than I thought." In this way, the instructor found himself obliged to make clear that he expected the "major paper" to be substantially longer than five pages, in the fifteen- to twenty-page range. He said later that at this point, he told students to plan "a good, healthy paper" featuring critical analyses from the assigned course readings "and at least three outside sources."

Phase Three: Term paper planning/composing
May 8–14

This revelation forced a rapid, major change in Mike's thinking about his term paper in the final week of classes. In this period, Mike had several final exams and end-of-semester deadlines for three papers, two of which were to be short—about five pages. The third was the paper on Amos, whose scope and length now posed a much larger challenge, since Mike had written few term papers of this length in previous courses. Now he scrambled to expand the scope of his task, since even at this late point "I had [only] a very rough outline, just a crude idea of what I wanted to do." He decided to follow what now seemed the most feasible plan, a section-by-section general analysis of a major theme in the text often discussed in the class, "the call of Amos and the day of Yahweh," to be followed by a comparison of this theme in other prophetic books. In this reformulation period, he met only briefly with the instructor to ask for a deadline extension. He completed the paper in two days of writing, just before the day when grades were due.

Though the paper was written under intense pressure, Mike was able to write what the instructor found to be a readable, clearly organized work that presented Mike's analysis of the primary text clearly. He noted that "your idea of organization and intertextual connections [within the Amos text] facilitated your exposition a good deal." In giving the paper an A, he wrote that "your paper is of high quality" and commented that "to proceed chapter by chapter" is often risky but that "you proved it can be done successfully."

There is a telling contrast between the American students' need to know a specific page total for their term papers and the German students' ability to read their instructors' unspoken expectations about their seminar papers. American readers will recognize the question "How long do you want this paper to be?" as a fundamental trope of American education. Mike believed it was the instructor's fault for not specifying the scope and page total of the paper: "The professor had a different idea than what the students had for . . . the assignment. . . . I suggested to him that the syllabus could have been more clear. You know it was a very lighthearted conversation."

Lighthearted or not, it is a conversation all too likely to recur in American classrooms. Precisely to avoid such confusion, the other American instructors in this study clearly spelled out page expectations for students to ensure no misunderstanding. This persistent need for instructors to define specific scope and length for most writing tasks suggests a systemic uncertainty about writing expectations in American undergraduate contexts. The variability of writing tasks in different composition courses, general education courses, and major courses in early semesters of study can leave American students unsure of their footing as academic writers and uncertain of their teachers' expectations for writing tasks. This uncertainty stands in clear contrast to the stability of expectations embedded in the German seminar contexts in this study. Questions about scope and length of seminar papers did not arise among the German students in this study, even though instructors' standards concerning task scope and length were never stated orally or in writing in the seminars. For the German students and instructors, the scope and length of seminar tasks appeared to be governed by tacitly shared knowledge of expectations and standards.

Table 3.2 Upper-Level Religious Studies Students

Text and Task Features	German Anja, 6th semester	American Mike, 6th semester
Task	seminar paper	term paper
Topic formation	15 weeks	14 weeks
Planning/research	5 weeks (full time in period between semesters)	5 days
Composing/revising	3 weeks (full time in period between semesters)	2 days (just before end-of-semester deadline)
Total task duration	23 weeks	15 weeks
Paper length	6,000 words	3,450 words

Task Patterns in Students' Work

The basic elements of German and American students' tasks in this study revealed contrasting patterns of planning and writing. Table 3.3 summarizes task patterns for all five pairs of case studies.

Table 3.3 Writing Task Patterns in Cross-National Comparison

Category	American	German
Time orientation	deadline oriented on-time productivity	composing autonomy open-ended productivity
Task pattern	short-burst planning/ writing limited recursiveness	extended planning/writing sustained, cumulative recursiveness

American patterns summarized in table 3.3 show the following key aspects:

- American students' writing processes were governed by the system mandate for on-time productivity.
- American students wrote in intense short bursts to meet paper deadlines.
- American students did only limited revising as they completed their papers.

Completion of all tasks by deadlines appeared to the American students to be the most important demand made of them as writers. They saw the ability to manage competing, fixed deadline pressures as a fundamental learning objective in developing their roles as writers.

In contrast, German students carried out seminar writing tasks not in response to deadlines but by means of self-initiated schedules governed by self-directed planning and research. The typical writing pattern in the German seminars consisted of a cumulative set of tasks including initial goal-setting and resource acquisition, ongoing resource analysis, and recursive writing and revising. German patterns in table 3.3 show these key aspects:

- German students directed their seminar tasks in keeping with their systemic autonomy and self-direction.
- German students spent months of reflection, study, and planning before beginning to write.
- German students believed that long-term task planning and development, as well as self-directed, free-time writing and revising, were their primary learning goals.

Authorship and Time in Students' Self-Perceptions

Table 3.4 summarizes time patterns for all five pairs of case studies.

Table 3.4 Writing Task Time Periods in Cross-National Comparison

Task Phase	American—Average Duration	German—Average Duration
Topic inquiry/formation	7 weeks	10 weeks
Planning/researching	Less than 1 week	5 weeks
Composing/revising	2 days	4.5 weeks
Total task duration	8 weeks	19.5 weeks

The disparities in the time patterns in table 3.4 are striking. German students spent an average of ten weeks shaping and reflecting on their topics during the regular work of their seminars, while American students spent about seven weeks developing their paper topics. The largest differences appeared in the planning and composing phases. German students spent five weeks on researching and text planning, while American students spent less than a week. American students' resources came primarily from course-related materials acquired by purchase, from handouts, or from library reserve; only Jill's seminar paper used sources acquired by active library or Internet search. Most notably, German students on average spent almost five weeks writing and revising their papers, while American students spent an average of less than two days composing their papers—including term papers.

By their own account, no American student in this study spent longer than three days actually writing a paper—most spending one or two days on all composing/revising activity. As table 3.4 shows, German students' average time for planning/researching/composing activities was over nine weeks, while the American students averaged about a week in these phases.

In connection with these system-specific practices, there were important differences between German and American students' awareness of time and their perceptions of their roles as writers. The American students interpreted the impact of time on their roles as writers negatively, as a constraint that limited task planning and information searches and compressed their composing/revising activity into narrow time frames. They equated time with pressure, necessitating the development of carefully targeted planning and composing strategies as coping mechanisms. Both Jill and Mike said that while they should have started planning and searching for resource materials sooner, it was their practice to construct tight schedules for most writing projects. They acknowledged that revision had little place in their composing schedules aside from quick editing for mechanics. Jill's motto—"It's all about due dates"—is indicative of their deadline-driven practices:

> A paper for English is due Monday, so I have Sunday to do that, and I have Monday night and Tuesday to write the paper for history, which is due Tuesday night. And, rather than being able to start a paper long before it's due, I find that I have too much due immediately . . . so it all gets blocked out to right before due dates for me.

Jill expressed a sense of lost opportunity as she considered the time-driven practices she had developed as an undergraduate:

> I wish I would have more time to spend on the papers. . . . I think the writing I produce would be a lot better if I could spend the time. If I had the time to do multiple drafts, I'd pick up on all the things, the little things, that I missed before.

The ambivalence in her statement "I wish I would have more time" suggests Jill's divided sense of authorship: while recognizing the limiting effects of her deadline-oriented writing practices, she believes that the system leaves her little choice if she is to succeed as a student.

Other American students echoed Jill's perceptions of time. Mike noted ruefully that "this is a lesson I've been learning over and over again: that I don't allow myself enough time to do papers. . . . Next semester," he concluded, "I think I'll take more time . . . because I've just left everything hanging until the end." Mike's description of the constraints of his writing practice is repeated in the narratives of other American students in this study—but not always with Mike's level of dissatisfaction. For example, Toni described how she begins to "think about the topic" and "do more brainstorming" as a paper deadline nears, "but I won't plan out how much time it will take to flesh out this idea until, like, two days before the paper's due. . . . [Then I] find a way to quickly get out, quickly get the project done." Toni was a self-assured writer who recognized the impact of the deadline-driven practices she had skillfully mastered: "I like to write; I just don't know when to get started." She acknowledged the limiting effect of her short-burst composing on the scope of her papers: "I have a really good time of getting to the point when I am pressured, without digressing . . . but they always end up being shorter papers." Toni was confident that she had mastered the short-term planning and deadline-driven composing that had brought her success as an academic writer.

American students reported discomfort with the limited scope of some of their writing tasks as well as with the short-burst composing practices they had learned to use. Sarah learned from her first paper that she had to limit the scope of her planned arguments in order to complete her assignment sequences on time. Reflecting on her first paper, she decided the small range of the assignment's primary-text basis—"about three pages of the document"—was not sufficient to justify the claim she had wanted to make: "You just use the document. . . . If you had a little more length you might have a little more information to pull from. . . . If the source is longer, you know, [it] might give away more information." In later papers she carefully restricted her argument to the scope of the assigned texts. Mike was not happy with the effort he put forth in his paper about the book of Amos. Given the freedom by a tolerant instructor to choose when and under what circumstances to shape his paper topic and seek planning guidance, he was unable to muster the self-discipline necessary to respond to his instructor's invitations to meet with him and plan his paper, even in the last weeks of the course. In retrospect, he said, he wished he had taken the time to reorganize his approach and focus more intensively on specific formal issues in the book of Amos: "Given the opportunity to write the paper again, I would take a different approach. [I] would come up with topics to be discussed in Amos . . . and discuss [them] by pulling from the book in the order that I saw fit." Yet, though Mike regretted how hastily he had planned and written his final paper, his short-burst skills enabled him to produce a clearly organized, well-styled paper that pleased his instructor. Like Jill and Toni, he carefully calculated the minimal time needed for his task. With the good grade in his hand, it is understandable that Mike perceived his deadline-driven planning/writing process as the most efficient use of his time under the circumstances.

While the American students viewed time as a constraint to be dealt with through carefully targeted compositional strategies, the German students tended to interpret time positively as representing opportunity, choice, and responsibility. Valuing free-time writing because "it gives you a lot of freedom," Kirsten wrote her paper between semesters in April after months of reading, discussion, and outlining during the regular semester. Anja also saw time as an opportunity for in-depth study:

> I feel good about doing work during this period [the free time]; it's a period when you can work for yourself on a topic, do your own research. I think that's what uni[versity] should be about. You develop the ability to work on your own, to work academically on your own.

However, Vera's reflections on her experience suggest the double-edged potential of free-time composing in the German environment.

She acknowledged that the practice of free-time writing kept her from receiving timely feedback from the instructor:

> You sit at home alone and you have nobody who knows about your topic who you can talk with. Normally you don't have anybody near you who can tell you this is bad structure, this is not the required way of citing, so you have to do it all on your own. And you have to force yourself to make progress and keep on doing it.

Vera's pattern demonstrated the expectation for self-direction embedded in the practice of free-time writing. Since she "hadn't read a lot about the problem of how to control the working class [in Socialist countries]," Vera went immediately in early October to her instructor to choose a topic and begin her planning. She gathered and read sources and began writing in the middle of December, slowly composing and revising each section: "I did a general revision after I had finished writing the whole paper." This deliberate, carefully structured process resulted in a completed paper as required on the final day of the regular semester in February.

Rhetorical Stance and Voice: Writing as Knowledge-Makers

Consider the notably different authorship practices articulated by Kirsten and Mike as they developed their term paper projects:

> I just sat in front of the shelf in the library and went through every volume of this journal to check if any titles were of interest to me. . . . I found a lot of great material and also some books, which I could use. (Kirsten)

> My process is to come up with a topic and then to go back to the [primary] text being used, to look for evidence of my thesis or things that correspond to that. You are [also] supposed to include class discussion and previous readings in the class in the paper. (Mike)

Kirsten, working on her paper for a lower-level history proseminar, decided to study the role of the Communist Party in prewar Nazi Germany. Searching for material related to this topic, Kirsten spent hours in the library poring over history books, journals, and archives. She did what an active knowledge-maker in her field would do: read widely and opportunistically to gain a sense of the broad context of her chosen topic. She understood that to get a sense of the complexity of the topic, she needed to learn more about current views on the issues. In her paper, she wanted to develop her own point of view in clear relation to some of the more strongly held, ideologically split arguments she had already encountered.

Mike represents a different approach to writing and knowledge-making. His assignment was to write a term paper about an Old Testament prophetic book—here the book of Amos—from any perspective he chose. He developed his project by learning the critical methodology his instructor had taught students to use, while reviewing issues raised in class discussion and other course readings. He did not see it as necessary to read widely in published discussions of others' views about his topic or to position his own views amid different, competing interpretations. Rather, his goal was to develop a well-crafted presentation of his own viewpoint, framed carefully in the methodological approach he had been taught. In these two episodes may be seen the patterns of authorship and knowledge-making characteristic of the two learning/writing environments in this study.

To clarify these differing patterns, I describe the work of the same two pairs of students as in the first section of this chapter—upper-level history majors Vera and Jill and upper-level religious studies majors Anja and Mike. (See tables 3.5 and 3.6.) Other students will be mentioned in the discussion that follows but will not receive detailed descriptions.

German: Vera

Entitled "The Worker and Labor Union Movement of Cuba from 1959 to 1973" ("Die Arbeiter- und Gerwerkschaftsbewegung Kubas von 1959 bis zum 1973"), Vera's paper treats the changes in Cuban workers' material situation and attitudes during the revolution. It is organized into a three-part structure, beginning with an introduction to connections between Cuban workers and Castro's economic policies, moving through several sections covering post-revolutionary changes in labor policies, and closing with her own conclusions. Vera relates her views to those of established historians, often citing a particular historian's position in order to move beyond that position:

> Because most workers were little politicized and had little experience in political resistance, their only alternative was to voice protests in the workplace. Goldenberg [an established scholar] writes in this connection that "the 'worker's state' of the intellectuals separated itself from that which the workers strove for." But in fact more radical forms of resistance [by workers] developed, when many goods were rationed due to failed economic planning.

In the conclusion, she finds that "the moral incentives [of the revolution] were not alone enough to motivate the workers," a view she acknowledges as confirming the critique of Cuban labor policy by several historians.

Vera's authorial voice combines a careful awareness of competing views with a deliberately impersonal tone, reflecting the "objectivity" she said she believes a seminar paper requires. Her strategy is shaped by what she remembered as her teacher's displeasure at earlier efforts to construct a personal voice. She described one this way: "[In earlier papers] I was just very free, I wrote something like, 'I think this and this,' which you are not supposed to say in [an academic] paper. . . . You are not supposed to give your personal view." Vera's belief that she should avoid a "personal view" led her to articulate opinions—both others' and her own—in a detached style that sometimes blurs differences among the viewpoints. For example, in the final sentences of the section on the revolution's class orientation, she says that "the non-elite mass of workers did not share power [with the leftist elite]. Accordingly the Castro regime could scarcely be put in the category of an underclass-supported populist regime." The hesitant phrase "could scarcely be put" suggests that she *has* a viewpoint, but her neutral tone does not convey a personal voice. As a result, she does not state how she thinks the Castro regime *should* be defined. In the paper's final pages, she reaches for a broader view of economic issues, but her summary remains generalized.

American: Jill

The main focus of Jill's seminar activity was her second paper on anti-Semitic laws in Nazi Germany. There is a distinct contrast between Vera's instructor's insistence that students of history incorporate a range of different "perspectives and opinions" in forming their arguments and the emphasis of Jill's instructor on the interpretation of primary source material as the basis of the historian's authority. In constructing her point of view in her paper, Jill reflected her instructor's emphasis on a clearly developed, personal interpretation of her primary sources. Jill's instructor, an experienced professor, said too many students have a one-dimensional view of history, thinking of it "as something that's happened, that's concrete . . . and there's only one way to see it." To counteract this tendency, he urged students to develop their own interpretive perspective of the "historical event" by means of their own analytic processes: "All I want you to do is give your own analysis at this point. . . . Take a set of circumstances, experiences, and then analyze. It should be an opinion that is rooted in the historical event." Careful readings of primary sources were the main focus of his expectations for students: "The historian doesn't want students to go off and say, 'Imagine what happened in the past.' We want you to . . . go back to the sources. What are the sources telling you?"

Jill strongly internalized her instructor's emphasis on developing her own analysis of primary sources:

> Primary sources automatically get more authority than my own or even the secondary sources, because they are primary sources. . . . Those voices from the primary sources would have to be given the most authority, and those are the sources

that the paper would be based on. Those sources are what I build off of, what I take apart.

She summarized her teacher's expectation this way: "Primary sources [are] what, you know, essentially you want to work with, just primary sources." For this reason, she chose a topic she thought could be based mostly on such sources: Germany's legislative treatment of the Jews from 1933 to 1939. This topic enabled her to use the texts of laws and contemporary news accounts as her main sources. But even though she ceded major authority to primary sources, Jill was confident that her own interpretive voice would remain in rhetorical control of her argument and the primary sources:

> I'd like to think that, when I sit down to write the paper, I immediately begin with as much of my own voice as there will be. I can see a paper of mine being dominated by quote after quote . . . , but I don't think I'd let that happen. I think that I am too nervous about it. . . . I think that in explaining your [decisions] by arguing, it's your own voice.

She believed that in constructing her own interpretation of primary sources, she would be able to keep her voice in the foreground.

Jill's paper, entitled "Segregation of the Jewish People in Nazi Germany: Legislation of 1933–1939," opens with an overview of "patterns of past anti-Semitic views" as they emerged in the Nazi party's ideology and policies. She briefly traces anti-Semitism in Hitler's early speeches and writings, then describes anti-Semitic legislation up to 1939. Unlike Vera, who responds to various interpretive perspectives in her paper, Jill relies almost entirely on primary documents, including laws, policy memos, and newspaper accounts, skillfully combining primary source materials in her discussion of Nazi legislation. She writes in a neutral, third-person voice that serves as a controlling center for her analyses of the origins of this legislation, which is clearly articulated but makes little reference to others' views or to potentially contested issues. For example, describing the Jews' loss of citizenship, she writes that this de-citizenship placed the Jews in the category of state "guest" or rather a provisional alien within the limits of the state. It is interesting to refer back to the letter by Adolf Hitler quoted above where he explicitly refers to the Jewish people as "aliens living among us."

She cites only two interpretive views, first quoting a scholar's statement that "the Nazi destruction process did not come out of a void. . . . The anti-Semitic views of Hitler and the Nazi party were not original. Anti-Semitism had always been apparent." She does not suggest how this view might be—or has been—contested. Nor in her other source citation, a quote asserting that the Nazis "set out to create a new outlook," does she suggest why this statement might conflict with the earlier claim about Nazism's unoriginality and what this apparent conflict might indicate about the wider debates over Nazism's cultural roots.

Her stated intentions in relying strongly on primary sources reveal a similar ambivalence. When she quotes from Hitler's letters about his attitudes toward Jews, she does so, she said,

in order to make the topic believable . . . to include some background on the Nazi mentality, and Hitler himself, because, you know, the hierarchy of everything answers straight back to him. Every law that was passed, every camp that was set up, they all . . . came back to him.

She validates the use of Hitler's own words as a means of giving her interpretation believability, but she does not address the subtle issue of whether citing Hitler's words as the source of "every law . . . and every camp" might run counter to a broader cultural view of Nazism. Jill concludes by saying that "the aims that the Nazi had were far different than earlier aims of anti-Semitic movements. By 1939, expulsion was complete, elimination was to follow." But as before, she gives no indication that she wants to position her claim about Hitler's differentness in relation to other authoritative claims about the issue.

Table 3.5 Upper-Level History Text Features

Text and Task Features	German Vera, 7th semester	American Jill, 8th semester
Task	seminar term paper	seminar term paper
Length	8,000 words	4,000 words
Primary sources	3	6
Secondary sources	11	3
Primary citations	63	22
Secondary citations	32	3

German: Anja

Anja was enrolled in an upper-level religion seminar focusing on the New Testament gospel of John. Having no list of paper topics or assigned readings to guide her, Anja had wide freedom as a writer and knowledge-maker. The main goal of such seminars, said the experienced professor teaching the course, was to help students learn the "kind of work appropriate to constructing a particular topic" in the field of New Testament study. In the place of a course plan, each week the professor wrote the textual passage for the next week's discussion on the blackboard. Students wanting to write semester papers were expected to develop their paper topics sometime during the semester, but no deadline was set. Though Anja had decided that she would write the semester paper, she did not begin forming a topic until the end of the term. She wanted to discuss and reflect cumulatively on issues arising during the semester's meetings, and she knew she could research and write after the semester was over. She chose to write on the John 14:6 text and to build her own interpretation of the passage.

In her paper, "An Exegetical Study of John 14:6 with Related Comparison of Selected Commentaries" ("Eine exegetische Untersuchung von John 14:6 mit anschliessendem Vergleich ausgewählter Kommentare"), Anja positions her interpretations clearly within the context of authoritative interpretations, noting her differences with

them. For example, diagramming the syntax of the Greek construction "the way and truth and light," she says that

> it is clear that all three predicate nouns are bound together in
> a row and in the same way to the subject *"e odos kai e aletheia
> kai e zoe."* Here Bultmann [a dominant commentator], who
> holds that the "ego" is the predicate rather than the subject,
> must be contradicted.

But because (as she noted in her journal) the professor had invited
seminar members "to prove from the text that your feeling and interpretation is right," Anja boldly foregrounds her own interpretation in
the final section, where it contrasts with established views. For the
first time in the paper—up to this point, she adopts a careful third
person style in handling the exegesis and analysis—she uses the first
person to assert the independence of her own interpretation: "It was
a surprise to me that in none of the commentaries on John 14:6 did
I find indications of the interpretation I have worked out. Nevertheless I prefer to differentiate my own position clearly from those of the
other commentators."

Waiting for the paper to be returned (it was handed back two
months later), Anja was enthusiastic that the professor had encouraged
her to develop an independent interpretation: "This is something I can
really put myself in." But in his comment on the paper, the professor dismissed her interpretation by saying that it was "unfortunately
mistaken," a view he reinforced in his marginal comments. She concluded that despite his professed interest in her own view, he had in
fact been unable to tolerate a novice's interpretation that went too far
beyond established views: "I thought, well, I've got certain points that
sort of argue for my opinion, and . . . the professor . . . said, 'I like
your approach, it was very independent, but I didn't like the result.'
And I thought, that doesn't make much sense to me!" Yet she was
"pleased" with her paper "even though the professor . . . chang[ed] his
opinion" of her own interpretive effort. She felt that she had learned
a valuable lesson about interpretive complexity in the field of New
Testament theology:

I always found different shades to it, and that was very interesting. . . . It was a never-ending story because there's mo-
ments when I find, oh yeah, this is also something that could
be related. So you never really come to an end; it's a process
of ongoing development.

Despite her disappointment, the project gave a strong boost to her
self-confidence as a participant in her chosen field.

American: Mike

In his course on the prophetic books of the Old Testament, Mike
decided to do a straightforward, section-by-section analysis of the
themes and forms of the text of the book of Amos. Mike's interpretive claims are grounded in his own textual analysis and make little
mention of other interpretations of Amos. "Everything I have read
[in the assigned texts] seems to be in agreement," he said later, and
"I didn't find nor did I look for a text that would disagree with what
was being said by the other authors."

The paper uses primary sources almost exclusively, with only a
few interpretive citations (four in twelve pages) used as support for
analytical generalizations rather than sites of interpretive difference.
Like Jill, Mike uses an impersonal authorial voice that centers on
his own viewpoint with only brief references to other views cited
in support of his own. For instance, Mike says that "the delivery of
the eight oracles is another example of the high literary merit found
in the book of Amos. Ward supports this view, 'this is perhaps the
most memorable group of oracles on foreign nations in the Hebrew
Bible' (Ward, 202)." The paragraph ends with this quote; there is no
further elaboration of Ward's view—how it might differ from other
views, or in what specific ways it supports Mike's analysis. In the final
pages, Mike begins a paragraph with a brief quote in support of his
concluding analysis:

Benedict de Spinoza writes, "the style of prophecy also varied
according to the eloquence of the individual prophet." The

idea [is] that Amos' message would be framed around the fact that he was a shepherd. There are several passages in Amos that lend themselves to this thesis.

There is no elaboration of how Spinoza's general point connects with Mike's analysis. The final paragraphs ends with the reiteration that the book of Amos is a work of "high literary merit." However, the instructor found the paper clear and well-organized and judged that it satisfied his expectations.

Table 3.6 Upper-Level Religious Studies Text Features

Text and Task Features	German Anja, 6th semester	American Mike, 6th semester
Task	seminar paper	term paper
Length	6,000 words	3,450 words
Primary sources	6	1
Secondary sources	13	3
Primary citations	Hundreds	40
Secondary citations	33	4

Connecting Writing and Knowledge-Making

These analyses suggest significant contrasts in German and American students' approaches to the connections between authorship and knowledge-making.

Table 3.7 Writing Roles and Rhetorical Stances in Cross-National Comparison

Category	American	German
Rhetorical stance	Author's voice representing individual authority in dominant, uncontested position	Author's voice representing relational authority responding to multiple, competing others

Table 3.7 indicates that German students constructed authority intersubjectively through an incorporative dynamic. Aware of their

instructors' expectations for a multiperspective approach in their discussions, German students drew widely on existing disciplinary conversations about issues and problems. For the American students, on the other hand, knowledge-making took textual shape as a series of analytic moves toward a dominant individual viewpoint. The American students constructed their arguments and analyses almost entirely in relation to primary texts, with very limited attention to established or competing views on the issues. They saw little place for themselves in broader conversations about competing perspectives.

This contrast suggests the importance of helping students at the undergraduate level articulate how they may wish to construct and hold knowledge. In recent years, efforts to define knowledge-making expectations for students have created an oppositional set of terms. The work of student writers, shaped by school traditions, is sometimes described as presenting the known and the given rather than constructing "new" knowledge. This distinction is often inscribed in critiques of inexperienced college students' writing: for example, Robert Davis and Mark Shadle suggest that new students too often display "the recording of existing knowledge" rather than "the creation of knowledge" in their writing, so that the "research paper" becomes "an apprentice work piecing together what is known . . . at least by the teacher" (425). This way of characterizing students' predispositions as academic writers inscribes an oppositional relationship between "existing knowledge"—the "given"—on the one hand and "new" or "created" knowledge on the other. This polarity runs the risk of oversimplifying issues of knowledge-making in academic fields. Legitimation processes differ widely among fields. In no field is there a simple opposition between the known and the new. The term "new knowledge" seldom has a stable meaning in any field; it has significance only in relation to how the "known" is held and validated by participants in the field.

For this reason, undergraduates should be drawn as fully as possible into ongoing conversations that define knowledge-building expectations in specific discursive contexts. It is tempting to assure uneasy undergraduates in their early semesters that they will not be expected to claim "new knowledge" in their papers but only to give their "own opinions" about issues. Yet such assurances not only reinforce their perceptions of their boundary status as knowledge-community participants but also may patronize their emergent recognition of complexity and connectedness in specific knowledge fields. It may make undergraduates reluctant to connect their own thinking with the complexities of disciplinary conversations.

This reluctance is illustrated in the differing approaches to historiography practiced by the German and American students in this study. While Vera demonstrates a constructivist approach to history, positioning her views within contexts of competing truth-claims, Jill emphasizes what Dominick LaCapra calls a "documentary" approach, relying on individual analysis of primary texts as the basis of historical inquiry. She elaborates her own perspective clearly but gives little attention to other voices and competing or contested claims. This emphasis on primary text analysis, says LaCapra, represents a "documentary or self-sufficient research model" based on the premise that historical knowledge consists of "primary (often archival) documents [that] enable one to derive authenticated facts about the past which may be recounted in a narrative . . . [and the goal of writing] is to be transparent to content or an open window on the past" (148–49). Such an orientation toward primary sources is not restricted to Jill's writing. Both Mike's treatment of the book of Amos and Kevin's presentation of the Serbian national viewpoint are also based on direct analyses of primary sources. Mike refers to other scholarly views on Amos only to support his own approach, not to cite differences.

A tendency to center controlling authorial voices in dominant, uncontested positions in analyses and arguments has been demonstrated in other studies of American students as well. For example, Geisler notes that the undergraduates in her study failed to establish connections in their analyses between their own views and other, established views on the topic. One student "spent the majority of her reflecting time" developing her own views and "tried to construct her position with little attention given to the positions of the authors she had read" (183). This feature of the undergraduates' writing in Geisler's study also is demonstrated in the writing of the experienced students in this study, like Jill in history and Mike in religion. Indeed, Jill's preference for constructing interpretations only from personal readings of primary sources re-articulates her instructor's emphasis on primary sources: "It's a skill I should've been practicing long before that last semester. . . . Primary sources [are] what essentially you want to work with. So to find something . . . that has the right date on it . . . it's really a whole lot of fun." Her view is also shown in Mike's comments on his developing beliefs about the study of biblical texts:

> I'm definitely learning that the best commentary on the Bible is the Bible itself. You have a unique literature there [be]cause it is a question of many books [in the Bible] . . . covering similar topics and sometimes [each book] takes a different approach.

Mike's comments suggest that he prefers doing his own direct comparative readings of biblical texts rather than incorporating broader interpretive conversations in Bible studies.

The differences in rhetorical outcomes are clear. The texts produced by American students are, for the most part, well-constructed, coherent analyses, relying on consistent analytic techniques with careful compositional attention. They develop clear authorial positions in their analyses, exemplifying skill in developing the essayist voice that Kurt Spellmeyer terms "a process of appropriation" by the writer (108). At the same time, their texts operate within narrow intersubjective horizons, seldom identifying other voices or views and then only for the purpose of supporting their own arguments and judgments. The consequences of this approach appear, for example, in Jill's unwillingness to identify or interrogate contested views about Nazi policy and cultural influences as she constructs her single-view conclusions about the cultural roots of Nazi anti-Semitism. It also appears in Mike's reluctance to offer any other perspectives outside his own analysis of textual features in the book of Amos.

On the other hand, students' strong efforts to incorporate other views can neutralize their own authorial voices, especially for inexperienced German writers. Jana's text for her first-semester proseminar in political science shows what can happen when an inexperienced writer follows a scholarly approach without knowing how to develop her own voice. Jana's text is both dominated and voiceless, a skillful synthesis with no authorial position—the primary risk of the *wissenschaftlich* tradition for students. In her paper, "The Universality of Human Rights," she creates a broad, skillfully narrated synthesis of established views of human rights movements in Christian and Islamic contexts. In conclusion, Jana tries briefly to articulate her own viewpoint but achieves only a derivative generalization: "People who define rights within a Christian context [as though] they could be defined the same way in an Islamic culture, are the chief obstacle to finding a [universal] ethos." To students like Jana, disciplinary conversations may appear to offer no entry point, giving her no space to locate her own voice. More experienced students, however, are often better able to demonstrate their awareness of what David Bartholomae calls "the forces at play in the production of knowledge" ("Writing with Teachers" 66). This awareness is most evident in the writing of Vera and Anja, who immerse themselves in the conversations among established authorities in their topic areas, shaping their own viewpoints within the larger contexts of competing truth-claims.

Students' Perceptions of Their Roles as Learner/Writers

There was a clear contrast in the ways the American and German students connected their practices as writers with their roles as novice participants in knowledge communities. The American students perceived themselves primarily as skillful producers of texts whose mastery of deadline-oriented production processes was the crucial index of their success as students. However, they made only tentative connections between their compositional masteries and their status as participants in academic discourse communities. Jill, for example, articulated her confidence in her ability to write effective texts under pressure. As a result of her senior seminar paper, she said she had "a lot more confidence in myself as a writer because . . . I know I can get the job done, and I can say what I need to say, clearly, effectively, and somebody can understand it." Yet, while acknowledging that being an effective writer was important for the study of history, she was guarded about the connections between her success as a writer and her status as a novice historian:

> When you start to write about [history], it makes you examine both yourself as a writer and . . . the topic at hand. . . . That's when, you know, if I could have spent more time, that'd be great. And I would've felt better about it, but I think that's more difficult.

Mike was satisfied that his efforts on his Amos paper had helped him become a better academic writer: "I think my ability is there to write at a high academic level; that ability just needs to be honed a bit and that will only happen by doing. So I just feel that the class has sharpened my skills a bit. But then there's still a lot more sharpening to do." However, though at the end of his third year, he remained uncertain about his progress as a religious studies major: "There's a whole discipline there that I haven't explored, and I'm just picking up the tools to explore that discipline." Mike felt himself still on the edge of the discursive field of religious studies.

Comparing Systems and Students

The results of a system encouraging short-burst writing practices were evident in the American students' work patterns. They saw themselves as obligated to maintain on-time writing productivity as they planned and wrote their papers. This finding suggests that the deadline orientation of the American semester carries a cost. Despite suggestions that they are a necessary evil—"All students need (even if they do not appreciate) the structure imposed by deadlines for meeting academic requirements" (Herrington and Curtis 381)—deadlines appeared to the American students in this study as a constraint that limited task planning and information searches. These constraints encouraged students to ration their attention to others' voices and views and to give most attention to building their own arguments in the limited time they gave to their tasks. Yet at the same time, the emphasis on shorter writing tasks and recurrent deadlines also made it possible for American students to receive more formative responses and feedback to their writing during the semester than did German students, especially in lower-level courses. Because the American students had several short writing tasks submitted, read, and returned during the semester, the feedback received on early assignments helped shape students' efforts on later assignments. This frequency of responsiveness had a distinct effect on students' progress in mastering compositional strategies during the semester. This was evident in Jill's reformulation of her writing goals for her second seminar paper, made in response to her instructor's comments on her first paper, and in her effort to articulate clearly her own viewpoint of Nazi anti-Semitic laws in the second paper. It was also evident in Sarah's ability to narrow her focus and tighten her arguments in her lower-level history course as she responded to her instructor's responses to the first few papers of the semester.

At the same time, these formative responses were received by students primarily in the context of text production, as feedback aimed at producing more effective textual structures. There is little evidence that their mastery of textual practices had a significant effect on their responsiveness to other's viewpoints or on their sense of participation as writers and knowledge-makers in specific fields. Thus, while gaining confidence as writers, the American students reflected uncertainty about their roles as participants in communities of knowledge.

In contrast, the German students framed their writing as part of their progress as knowledge-makers in their disciplines. They showed strong awareness of their authorial roles as knowledge-makers in their discourse communities. At the same time, the tradition of free-time writing limited German students' opportunities to seek formative responses from instructors or peers during the drafting and revising stages of their work. They received feedback from instructors and peers mostly during the planning stages but worked largely alone during the free-time periods between semesters. As a result, the feedback they received during the composing/revising stages came mostly from peers available during free-time periods rather than from experienced teachers.

These findings suggest both strengths and weaknesses in each system in relation to students' writing as knowledge-makers. To be successful in their seminars, German students must learn to sustain independent, goal-driven planning, researching, and writing as they develop their projects. The seminar system challenges them to work as active knowledge-makers in specific fields from the beginning of their university study. The pattern of between-semester composing, however, often means that they write and revise their texts without much formative feedback from instructors or classroom peers. For American students in this study, on the other hand, the evidence suggests that the orientation to on-time productivity built into undergraduate settings has divergent effects. It produces confident writers capable of completing short-term writing tasks with efficient, well-managed composing strategies. But at the same time, it limits students' motives for developing writing practices characteristic of experienced participants in knowledge communities—in particular, self-directed, goal-driven planning and researching, reflective composing/revising, and the construction of intersubjective authority as writers.

The following chapters will propose ways to strengthen students' roles as writers and knowledge-makers. Proposals will draw on the strengths of both systems and will address American teachers and students. If American undergraduates are to learn to write as knowledge-makers and to undertake self-directed, goal-driven planning, writing, and revising more consistently, they must be challenged with the appropriate expectations. Additionally, American teachers should heed Kathleen Blake Yancey's proposal for more reflectiveness in American writing classrooms—"the dialectical process by which we develop . . . specific goals for learning" and "strategies for reaching those goals" (6). These possibilities for change will be explored at length in the next three chapters.

4 / Shaping Transformative Writers: Priorities for Change

Teachers typically assess students' writing in terms of their individual or group output; how might we describe students' success as writers in terms of the systems in which they work? As previous chapters show, the German and American students in this study defined success as academic writers in different ways. The German students entered university as participants in two or three specific knowledge fields, taking on an autonomy that allowed them wide freedom as academic writers. During their seminars, they formulated long-term, self-directed reading/writing projects, continuously revising and elaborating their perspectives during the semester and completing extended papers largely during postsemester lecture-free time. Their success depended upon whether they could sustain the self-directed process of planning, researching, drafting, and revising their seminar papers consistently to their conclusion. The American students took on quite different roles. Instead of beginning as learner/writers in a few major fields, they had to meet the twin demands of composition and general education. In response to these challenges, they developed two parallel writing roles in early semesters: as writers in composition courses and as novice—and temporary—learner/writers in several different disciplinary areas from the general education array. They produced a variety of texts at frequent deadline points during the semester to achieve success in these contexts.

In their first-year writing courses, the American students wrote a variety of (mostly short) papers on topics related to the varied interests of their courses. In their general education courses, they wrote quizzes, short papers, and exams linked to specific, time-limited units of study as they articulated basic concepts and wrote briefly in a few discipline-specific styles and genres. What students primarily learned as writers in general education writing was that academic success required practices that produced focused, clearly organized texts formulated within efficient, on-time production sequences. All of the American students in this study had achieved some measure of academic success by learning to produce texts in a timely manner. The American students freely acknowledged that the price of this productivity was a lack of revision of their texts. Once they began planning and writing, they composed rapidly in completing their tasks. Facing multiple, diverse writing tasks at specific deadlines during a semester, they used what they saw as just sufficient time to plan, organize, draft, and edit their texts in a sequence that matched the delivery dates. Though topic-formation times varied by student and task, the evidence in chapter 3 suggests that students spent a week or less on planning and writing, including term papers. Because they had learned to produce clearly written, well-organized texts during short, intensive drafting periods, they did not perceive it as necessary to leave much time for reworking or revision. The more experienced students in their later semesters—Jill, Mike, and Toni—had learned that if they began with a general idea of their topic, they could plan, organize, and complete a text of ten or more pages within a few days.

The American students certainly did not learn short-burst writing from teachers. Most had been taught to revise texts in high school writing courses, and all had learned recursive writing processes in their first-year writing courses at Midwestern. And though Midwestern University had no formal writing-across-the-curriculum program, several teachers in disciplines other than English in this study had participated in university-wide seminars in which revision strategies were extensively explored. Consequently, these teachers had constructed course schedules that invited students to engage in process-based planning and composing. Though only one syllabus in this study contained specific recursive activities, all teachers invited students to plan, draft, and revise over time on their own. For this purpose, topic selection guidelines and paper deadlines were clearly charted on course syllabi, with weeks between task deadlines. Most course schedules announced tasks and possible topics at the beginning of the semester, and except in Sarah's course (which featured a sequence of short papers) allowed weeks between topic selection and paper due dates. Only in Sarah's course, with its sequence of discrete, short papers, did the instructor specifically invite students to revise and resubmit papers, though Sarah revised only one paper briefly. Yet despite their earlier experiences as revising writers and despite the opportunities to reflect and revise offered by their course structures, the students in this study had learned to rely on the intensive, short-burst strategies that had emerged as the basis of their writing roles by the time they participated in this study.

Although the American students in this study perceived short-burst composing as essential to their academic success, they were acutely aware that these practices ran counter to what they had been taught. Several acknowledged that they wished they had found the time to work recursively but admitted they found it impossible to do so. How did this come to be?

"It's All About Dates": Recursiveness and Short-Burst Writers

One answer implicates the American academic system itself: students had discovered that they didn't need to revise because they could write well-styled, clearly organized papers that satisfied instructors without revision. To them, recursiveness came to seem a systemic liability, since readable, well-organized papers delivered on precise deadlines were the outcomes most valued by their system. To be sure, students had learned in writing courses that revision could help produce more complex, reflective papers. But gradually they also learned that sharply focused short-burst strategies could produce well-written papers that satisfied teachers. They had, like Toni, come to see themselves as skillful practitioners of point-to-point text production: "I like to write," she said; "I just don't know when to get started." Yet once started, "I find a way to quickly get out, quickly get the project done." Recursiveness gradually lost importance among the practices Toni and the others in this study saw as essential to successful academic authorship. While they allowed that recursiveness was desirable, they did not see the need to practice it.

So while the American system of time-driven text production may be part of the picture, an important question remains: How is it that these students so readily bypassed the recursive practices they had been taught repeatedly in school and early college semesters? To confront this question, it is essential to consider how these students may have learned revision and the pedagogy that framed this learning. Indisputably, recursiveness and revision have been traditional elements of composition instruction in American education. They have been taught as key practices by generations of American writing teachers and textbooks, and scholar/teachers have made strong and persuasive arguments on behalf of a practice-based pedagogy of revision. Rachel Martin, for example, explains how she teaches revision practices to her students:

> I write revision on the board and ask people to identify the root word and then the entire meaning . . . defining revision as the point at which you step back and resee your own ideas. In doing so, maybe you realize that what you really want to say comes out only at the very end of the first draft. . . . Adding, crossing out, rearranging, and starting over all become possibilities for a next move. It becomes clear that revision is really the heart of composing. (86)

Martin continues by describing the extensive revision steps through which she leads her students as they write. In another context, Joseph Harris has argued that revision should be taught as "a new sort of intellectual *practice*" (original emphasis) which would bring "a renewed attention to the visible practice or labor of writing" ("Revision" 577–78). If we want "to teach writing as a practice," he adds, "revision is key" (578). Harris elaborates his point (to which I will return shortly) by outlining a course in which the labor of revision itself gives shape to writing as a "*project*—a cluster of defining concerns and interests . . . a point to move toward" (588; original emphasis). He suggests that teachers should teach "the actual labor of drafting, revising, and editing texts" (591). To illustrate his argument, he tells of several students' ongoing efforts to rethink and revise their writing as part of a sequence of drafts built into the structure of the course.

In this view, well argued by Martin, Harris, Amy Lee, Yancey, and others in the tradition of revision studies, students learn recursiveness best when it is taught as practice—as a set of activities aimed at rethinking and revising text. And indeed, as the studies and arguments cited here show, a practice-oriented revision pedagogy can bring complex, nuanced textual outcomes when applied in specific course settings. Behind this broad tradition is, I think, the conviction that if cumulative rethinking and revision are taught forcefully as basic practices, they will become embedded in students' roles as writers in their disparate knowledge communities. Yet the attitudes and practices of the students in my study suggest that recursive thinking, planning, and writing taught as basic practices may not easily persist in the broader undergraduate curricular environment.

Recursiveness and Students' Roles as Transformative Writers

Here is what we know: the teaching of recursive writing practices has been an essential aspect of American writing pedagogy. The students in this study had practiced recursive thinking/writing processes in their composition courses and acknowledged that they saw recursiveness as a desirable element in planning and writing. Yet recursive practices did not systematically carry over into their writing roles in courses beyond composition. The students in this study—including Toni, the senior English/journalism major, the most practiced writer of the group—came to believe that the operations of planning, composing, revising, and editing could be streamlined efficiently into rapid-drafting, quick-editing text-production strategies, well adapted to the intermittent tasks and deadlines in their course schedules. This disconnect between composition experience and subsequent writing practice suggests that recursiveness is conditioned by several factors that affect a practice-based pedagogy of revision:

- Recursive processes may not be consistently portable between writing contexts with different expectations and tasks.

- Students do not necessarily practice recursiveness if successful outcomes—on-time productivity and teacher satisfaction—can be achieved without it.

• Recursiveness, defined as sustained, cumulative, self-directed rethinking and revising, develops as part of a complex of intentions embedded in students' broader writing roles.

These conditions suggest that unless students experience recursiveness as more than a specific set of revision practices aimed directly at text production, they may learn recursiveness more as local tactics than as long-term strategies. Sternglass observes that "composition instruction cannot be seen in a vacuum"; while it "is an important first step . . . composition instructors should not believe that they are the final influence, or perhaps even the most important influence, in the development of writing abilities" (141). The evolution of students' writing practices in this study suggests that recursiveness is gradually blended and shaped within the dynamics of writing roles developed in response to specific knowledge-community participation. That is, it seems clear that students' writing practices in this study developed as part of broader authorship roles, shaped through system imperatives, teacher expectations, and disciplinary patterns. Even years of practice-based revision instruction had little long-term sustainability for these undergraduates once they began writing as knowledge-makers in particular discursive contexts.

This perspective suggests that recursive practices, vital as experienced writers recognize them to be, are best learned by undergraduates as components of writing roles constructed within specific knowledge contexts. I formulate this view as follows: *Students will best learn sustainable, self-directed recursiveness in thinking and writing when they take on roles as transformative writers in a variety of knowledge-making contexts.*

What I am calling transformative writing is the key to this perspective. I use it as a collective term for the thinking and writing processes that enable students to write in the roles of knowledge-makers in specific knowledge contexts. Transformative writing changes the way students build and hold knowledge, enabling them to construct new forms of authority and develop new authorship roles. These processes include assimilating, critiquing, and responding to others' views and reconstructing personal views and voices in relation to them.

Transformative writing shares some of the qualities Linda Flower attributes to "rival hypothesis thinking," which emphasizes "the value of positing open questions, sustaining genuine inquiry, and interrogating evidence—both one's own and others'" (*Learning to Rival* 182). Transformative writing has a participatory dimension, because it is grounded in the motives, goals, and practices of specific knowledge communities. It draws students into reasoning strategies and discursive conventions of different knowledge fields—enabling them to recognize that, for example, the analytic techniques and rhetorical strategies of literary study differ from those in historical inquiry or social analysis.

Transformative writing has both social cognitive and subjective dimensions. In her extensive exploration of social cognitive knowledge-making, Flower speaks of meaning-making as a "constructive, transformative process" in which students negotiate meaning from the interplay of their own and others' views as they "learn a new discourse and its distinctive ways of making meaning" (*Construction* 103). From the cognitive perspective, says Flower, transformative knowledge-making entails both a social dimension (collaborative interaction) and "self-reflexiveness" (an awareness of the knowledge-building processes by which meaning-making unfolds) (296). In this perspective, transformative writing is a fundamentally social activity, requiring collaborative interaction to succeed. Through it, students build more complex and multivalent understandings of subject matter, including broader conceptual understandings and stronger command of analytic and interpretive strategies. It also encourages students' moves toward more multivalent and pluralist attitudes and opinions, as William Perry suggests in his model of undergraduate learning development.

In a subjectivist perspective, transformative writing enables students to experience the intersubjective basis of knowledge-making. Transformative writing draws on the idea of "mutuality," which David L. Wallace and Helen Rothschild Ewald describe as the basis of students' agency as knowledge-makers. In this view, students must be invited "to take subject positions as co-constructors of knowledge," based on reciprocal interactions between students and teachers (2).

To bring about mutuality in the classroom, Wallace and Ewald urge a pedagogy that "assume[s] learning begins at the intersection of students' knowledge and experiences and the teachers' representations of disciplinary knowledge" (17). From the interplay among shared horizons of knowledge comes the interaction that can build students' "interpretive agency"—students' capacity to bring "prior experience to bear in the construction of knowledge" (16). In this perspective, writing must be grounded in intersubjectivity. Intersubjectivity is not only the awareness of others' viewpoints but also, in Barbara Rogoff's words, a "social activity that can be regarded as the bridge between one understanding of a situation and another . . . that is, shared understanding based on a common focus of attention and some shared presuppositions that form the ground for communication" (71). Transformative writing acknowledges shared horizons, responds to others' perspectives, and identifies commonalities and differences as the basis of knowledge-making.

Students' Knowledge Communities: Enacting Roles as Knowledge-Makers

Transformative writing depends upon students' participation in communities of knowledgeable others. There are two important signifiers in this phrase—"community" and "knowledgeable others." The term "community" takes on multiple, overlapping meanings in relation to student participation. The apprenticeship model proposed by Jean Lave and Etienne Wenger offers a useful perspective for defining students' relationships to knowledge communities. Defining learning as "an integral part of generative social practice in the lived-in world," Lave and Wenger suggest the phrase "legitimate peripheral participation" to indicate "multiple, varied, more-or-less engaged and inclusive ways of being located in the fields of participation defined by a community" (36). While periphality itself can be a source of power or powerlessness, in proper frameworks it can be "empowering": "periphality, when it is enabled, suggests an opening, a way of gaining access to sources for understanding through growing involvement" (37).

The concept of the "learning community" in academic contexts reflects the values of participation and interaction in Lave and Wenger's model. Apprenticeship in an academic knowledge community is based on identification with the shared "attitudes, values, expectations, and practices" of the community, in the words of Nancy S. Shapiro and Jodi H. Levine (4). Experienced community members—teachers, researchers, advanced students—share the motives and expectations that drive discussion, critique, reading, writing, and publication. They will say to novice participants, as Gee says about historians, "If you want to study history, this is how we do it: this is how we think, this is how we act, these are our tools" (127). Through continuous interactions with experienced community participants, students begin to master the roles necessary for active participation as learner/writers in their communities.

The apprenticeship model, however, does not address crucial aspects of undergraduates' status as novice writers in knowledge communities. Undergraduates inherit a distinctive in-betweenness in their status. Unlike apprentices in professional and craft areas, undergraduates have immediate direct responsibility for their own work products and more freedom within which to produce them. They also have less monitoring by teachers or mentors. Indeed, the advantages of graduate-level status—mentoring and other participatory experiences—are often unavailable to undergraduates. Because of these constraints, the basic elements of genuine knowledge-community membership—community identification and authentic participation—are only partially available to undergraduates.

Indeed, what "community" means for undergraduates as writers has been much debated in composition studies—for example, in Bartholomae ("Inventing the University"); Trimbur ("Consensus and Difference in Collaborative Learning"); McCarthy and Fishman; Patricia Bizzell; and David Foster. It has been applied to established discourse networks of knowledge fields (Bartholomae) and to culturally diverse classroom groups seeking some commonality amid difference (McCarthy and Fishman). Both interpretations have value in thinking about undergraduate settings, but I want to specify two distinct but overlapping meanings as I use the term here. One interprets community as a discursive network of shared discourses, values, and methodologies into which students must write themselves:

> Every time a student sits down to write for us [teachers], he has to invent the university for the occasion. . . . He has to learn to speak our language, to speak as we do . . . to appropriate (or be appropriated by) a specialized discourse. (Bartholomae, "Inventing the University" 134)

As novice participants in special networks, students read, assimilate, discuss, cite, and respond to the authoritative voices of the network. They become familiar with the values and practices that drive the work they read, discuss, and write about. In this context, community signifies the cluster of concepts and practices that shape knowledge in a particular domain or area and that must be learned by newcomers if they are to have roles in the activities of the field.

In another sense especially important to undergraduates, "community" exists as the material and virtual spaces in which students interact in classrooms, small groups, tutorials, or on-line discussion groups. These are the daily "communities" students know on an intimate basis, featuring "the everyday struggles and mishaps of the talk in our classrooms . . . with their mixings of sometimes conflicting and sometimes conjoining beliefs and purposes" (Harris, *Teaching Subject* 107). These groupings are local institutional formations that interact with the broader networks of disciplinary networks. In this composite definition of knowledge community, students take on the roles of "knowledgeable others" as a function of their participation in these networks. They need not be experts to take on such roles—their beliefs, assumptions, and knowledge claims are functions of their participatory roles, no matter what their level of prior knowledge. Inexperienced students may have only a rudimentary knowledge of issues and terms, but they will share functional roles as knowledgeable participants. In this model, the key to a student-oriented knowledge community is intersubjectivity—the sharing of subjective horizons within specific knowledge fields. The goal of such participation is not agreement or consensus-building but encounter, discovery, and response within a setting of common interests. It is this participative context that enables students to write as knowledge-makers.

Writing tasks requiring immersion in the active conversations of specific knowledge communities will help students develop genuine authority as knowledge-makers. Extended writing tasks focused on specific topic areas will

- strengthen students' awareness of the relational nature of knowledge-making;
- encourage students to articulate a sense of self in relation to communities of diverse, competing voices;
- help students learn the obligation to listen, assimilate, and respond to other, different views and perspectives;
- help students master the rhetorical strategies needed for incorporating and responding to other viewpoints.

Writing to Build Expertise

American undergraduates are not consistently challenged to participate significantly in disciplinary (or interdisciplinary) communities. With most entering students facing various short-term general education obligations and with many undecided about major interests, undergraduates have little incentive in early semesters to engage fully in specific knowledge-area discourses. At the same time, undergraduate teachers may find themselves frustrated by students' persistent sense of outsiderness in relation to specific knowledge areas. Even the upper-level students in this study showed hesitation in describing themselves as full participants in their major knowledge fields. They did not see strong connections between their writing and their status as knowledge-makers in their major fields. In a long-term study of college students' writing development, for example, Sternglass finds that underprepared students had difficulties in meeting institutional writing "assessment" and "proficiency" standards and made little progress as writers in first-year composition courses (even remedial courses). A student she followed for several years began succeeding as an academic writer only when she began writing in her major courses, where she could "make connections between the insights of that field and other discipline areas and . . . apply her insights to real-world problems" (6). Her development as a writer began to flourish only when she began writing to make knowledge in her chosen field—that is, as she learned to build expertise in a special area. This indicates a synergistic relationship between writing development and knowledge-making that leads to expertise in specific areas.

It has been argued, however, that American undergraduates' development of expertise may pull them away from their personal literacy contexts and diminish their authority as writers. Geisler, for example, calls the space between boundary status and full knowledge-community participation a "great divide" that separates professionals with "expertise" who have mastered academic literacy practices from "novices of the academy" and "laypersons" who have not (88–92). Since academic literacies and expertise tend to be associated with the literacies of the "upper-class elites," says Geisler, students who write to make knowledge and gain expertise may be separated from the "culture of their everyday life" in the process (251). This view suggests that undergraduates' acquisition of expertise is inherently exclusivist, drawing them away from their family and community literacies. I believe that this argument has some validity, in the sense that students must go beyond their earlier literacy range as they learn to read and write within disciplinary discourses. But I also suggest that the "great divide" metaphor is misleading as a definer of learning space. Like the "existing knowledge/new knowledge" binary, the "great divide" figure implies that the spaces between boundary and center—those between lay or personal literacies and the discourses needed for expertise—are blocked by hurdles or barriers. Rather, I believe that these learning spaces are better described as pathways or networks. The transition from novice to active knowledge-maker is a continuum of growth experiences, seldom a single leap over a divide. In this sense, the "divide" metaphor makes it difficult to see that for undergraduates, "in-betweenness" may be a positive, ongoing developmental process. For this reason, the development of expertise is best represented as a strengthening of personal authority, not as the loss of it.

This view of expertise and its literacies as desirable goals for undergraduates is essential to the argument I want to make here—that undergraduates should be invited to write as active knowledge-makers in specific fields as early and as often as possible. Students can best develop their authority as transformative writers through frequent opportunities for active, intersubjective participation in communities of knowledge.

The "Authority" in Authorship

Students must discover the sociality of knowledge-making in order to build authority in knowledge communities. Lev Vygotsky's "zone of proximal development" signifies the developmental space at the borders of knowledge communities where learners can, "in collaboration with more capable peers," learn the literacy practices sponsored by specific knowledge contexts (86). It is this "zone" that offers students opportunities to move from the boundaries toward the active centers of disciplines as they learn how to analyze, critique, and compose knowledge claims in response to others' voices and views. As Bazerman maintains, undergraduates should be drawn as fully as possible into ongoing conversations that define knowledge-building expectations in specific discursive contexts. He urges teachers to build "courses that enable students to enter into disciplines as fully empowered speakers rather than as conventional followers of accepted practices . . . [so that] they can always keep in mind the fundamental goals of the fields" (79). It is tempting to assure uneasy American undergraduates that they will not be expected to speak and write as "experts" but only to give their "own opinions." But I have argued that this is a false dichotomy and that students must be challenged to learn the inquiry processes of specific knowledge fields in interaction with others, expert and novice, "placing their voices next to the voices of others," as Bruce Ballenger suggests (107). Indeed, the American students in this study were confident of their skill in constructing coherent analyses of issues and texts based on their own viewpoints. But even in their extended tasks, they acknowledged only a limited range of competing views on issues and seldom responded extensively to those views. They did not see their compositional skills—rewarding as they found them to be—as incorporated in collaborative knowledge-making. I believe that American undergraduates should encounter this challenge more actively and fully as they develop authority as academic writers. The nature of American undergraduates' authority as writers and knowledge-makers is the subject of ongoing debate in composition pedagogy. One view is reflected in Elbow's expressivist idea that first-year students should be encouraged "to write as though they are a central speaker at the center of the universe" ("Being a Writer" 80). This perspective suggests an individualist, I-centered authority based on personal knowledge and awareness. The inclination of the American students depicted in this book—veterans of high school and university writing courses—to rely on an I-centered stance in their writing suggests Alan W. France's assertion that "composition studies . . . is skewed toward agency, toward the personal experience of the world" (148). Proponents of this view argue that personal authority is crucial to new writers at university, offering them a secure space in the face of unfamiliar environments. It enables them to return to unexamined aspects of their own experiences and histories as they become aware of broader perspectives. It encourages them to recognize the range of their own untested attitudes and opinions about important issues. A personal voice in academic writing also represents a significant form of rhetorical agency, allowing students to connect new and unfamiliar discourses with familiar literacies developed from school and personal knowledge.

Another equally important view emphasizes the value of teaching students to write in sustained responsiveness to other, competing voices and views. This relational authority is the basis on which expertise is built. It requires students to begin learning a "new authority for generating knowledge," in the words of McCarthy and Fishman, bringing "a willingness to engage in a different sort of conversation with themselves and the multiple voices of others" (464). It requires students to construct textual voice as a "coherent, self-conscious identity [shaped] in order to . . . join discourse communities," in France's words (149). It depends on students recognizing the "role of rhetorical knowledge in the development of authority" and must be at the heart of the authority novice writers seek, suggest Ann M. Penrose and Cheryl Geisler (517). They maintain that students must "believe there is authority to spare—that there is room for many voices," because "knowledge develops through conversation and debate by actively analyzing authors' assumptions and motivations, and the situations in which they work" (517). This intersubjective authority is the essential building block of expertise, enabling students' active participation in disciplinary conversations. It requires students to learn new terms for new ideas and concepts, and new modes of argument and analysis for making knowledge claims. For students whose writing has been based primarily on a personal, I-centered authority, this relational, intersubjective authority can seem alienating. Students may see themselves as forced to produce—in Ballenger's words—"writing that is not their own" (15) or as operating temporarily in a discourse they can never master.

Undergraduates may conclude that they cannot achieve this relational authority—or that if they do, they must set aside their personal authority as writers to do so. Students may respond to this challenge by falling into a neutral voicelessness, allowing their voices to become blank pages filled out by others' words. The German students in this study were more vulnerable to this risk than were the American students because of the stronger priority given to recognizing established views inherent in the German scholarly tradition. Jana's paper on the idea of universal human rights (see chapter 3) shows this effect. It is also heard in the words of the Rhineland University student who believed she was "not given a chance to have an opinion" as she cited and responded to authoritative voices in her field. Yet her defiant assertion that "I have something to say and I want to find out if it is true" suggests a counteracting desire to affirm her own voice in connection with others. Her words express a stage crucial to an academic writer's growth: the development of what Ballenger calls "a sense of self, a belief—even if it is a temporary fiction—that their writing is their own" (15). Indeed, there is a special relationship between "ownership" and connectedness in the making of a novice writer's authority: to realize the authority of the individual voice, its relation to others must be heard and understood. This relationship is based on the "mutuality" and "reciprocity" that Wallace and Ewald define as "teachers and students sharing the potential to adopt a range of subject positions" (3). A sense of mutuality offers important grounding for novice academic writers as they explore the interactive demands of disciplinary participation.

Students should be encouraged to see this relational, intersubjective authority as an enlargement of personal authority rather than its effacement. It is not necessary to see the personal and the relational as conflicting; they are combinatory when the evolution of voice reflects the development of new authority. A student's relational authority, far from excluding the personal or the expressive, can best be grounded in a personal voice that acts as the controlling rhetorical center of a text. Herrington and Curtis point out that the students they observed engaged in a "self-authorizing" process in which they "used the drafting process as much to configure their identities in relation to their various subjects as to master the forms, genres, and language in which those subjects were conveyed" (383). Indeed, the personal dimension of the writer's voice is essential to what I am terming transformative writing, allowing the writer to manage multiple other voices and views from a stable center. Mark Richardson describes students' experiences in building their own literary interpretations to show that "teachers can facilitate students' use of their 'native languages' and their own knowledge and gradually bring them across the bridge that separates their knowledge from the privileged discourse of the academy" (282).

The interdependence of the intersubjective and the personal can clearly be seen in the students' texts cited in chapter 3. For example, Kirsten's strong personal voice grounds her perspectivist analysis of German Communism, allowing her to negotiate conflicting views and construct her own perspective in response. Equally striking is the impact of Anja's personal voice in its role as the authoritative core of a complex argument that positions her own viewpoint against several traditional views of a core New Testament passage. As an American example, Jill's strong—though impersonal—voice, in her analysis of the anti-Semitic legal system of Nazi Germany, binds the various strands of her argument clearly, though with little intersubjective awareness of others' positions. That fact that Jill understates the conflicts and competing positions in her topic suggests that she, like the other American students, relies on a personal perspective as the mainstay of her rhetorical authority in her text. But her personal perspective is clearly demonstrated as she negotiates the issues that underlie her thesis development.

Stepping into roles as active knowledge community participants is crucial if undergraduates are to experience a sense of authority writing as knowledge-makers. Russell notes that writing research "suggests again and again that when writing mediates further involvement with the activity—the social life—of the discipline, it is more successful for inviting students to go further intellectually and personally" ("Where" 283). In her long-term studies of students' writing development at college, Sternglass demonstrates repeatedly that specifically situated, rhetorically demanding writing tasks help students see themselves as active knowledge-makers able to "reflect on, analyze, and evaluate complex ideas" as active knowledge-community participants (59). Tasks requiring students to play the role of "professional-in-training," not merely "text processors," were found by Walvoord and McCarthy to be successful in helping students use the "knowledge and method-ology being taught in the course" to address "issues and problems" of the discipline (*Thinking* 9). These studies show that extended writing tasks can have a strong positive effect on students' sense of agency as writers and enhance their self-perceptions as insiders in specific knowledge fields.

Building Transformative Writing: Key Teaching Priorities

The basic qualities of transformative writing may be stated this way:

- Transformative writing is inherently self-directed and goal-driven, as students sustain learning progress in specific knowledge communities.
- Transformative writing is inherently recursive, requiring persistent, cumulative rethinking and revising within com-munities of knowledgeable others.

- Transformative writing requires students to develop rhetorical strategies that recognize the relational, intersubjective basis of knowledge construction.

These qualities require that students be challenged to find their voices in conversations that may be difficult to follow. Deferral and hesitancy are to be expected as students confront the demands of active participation. Finding their voices as writers in a dialectic that threatens their security will always seem risky and dangerous. It is a matter of entering "the dialectic between self and culture" in ways that allow students to perceive the constructedness of their own ways of seeing (France 155). It will not come easily to students new to an academic environment and comfortable with the construction of personal viewpoints. Only in response to clear expectations and direct challenges, says Robert P. Yagelski, will students "attempt to write themselves into the broader discourses that shape their lives," developing "writing roles" that validate their sense of self and moving gradually toward the authority that allows them to listen as well as to speak (93).

The following priorities should guide teachers' efforts to connect writing and knowledge-making in ways that help students develop transformative writing.

Priority One

Develop extended writing projects that emphasize self-directed, goal-driven planning, research, and writing.

To achieve this goal, teachers should encourage students to see a semester course as a set of opportunities driven by goals rather than by deadlines. An extended writing project will allow students to develop, change, reflect on, and reformulate their understandings as their reading, study, research or service activities, and writing dictate. To give space for change and indecision and to allow for the confusion and frustration inherent in sustained projects, opportunities for feedback and interaction should be maximized, and grading should be kept to a minimum during the semester. Teachers should recognize the tensions between student freedom and semester time pressures in their course structures. On the one hand, they can sequence project activities—forming topics, developing work plans, doing research and service activities, and drafting and revising—in a clear temporal framework. But these stages should also be identified as necessary elements of self-directed productivity. Students will readily perceive the time pressures built into each stage; they should also be encouraged to recognize the self-guided choices in each stage. As I note in the next chapter, this bit of pedagogical sleight-of-hand won't fool students, but it may help them recognize that developing roles as writers and knowledge-makers entails self-directed choices at each step. It may also encourage them to feel ownership for their goals and the strategies they choose to achieve them.

The learning goals and expectations outlined here are appropriate for composition courses and courses in specific disciplinary fields. Teachers must decide, of course, what specific courses are most suitable, but these goals are not limited to a particular course model or content. The only requirement is that the course be sufficiently flexible to incorporate an extended writing project based on self-directed, goal-driven activity. Many undergraduate courses may be too large for the necessary student-instructor interaction or may be driven by a coverage imperative leaving too little freedom for students' individual projects. Each decision will be local, reflecting learning goals and settings specific to teachers' situations. Freedom, self-direction, and reflectiveness will be the key features of students' learning experiences in these courses.

The "Outcomes Statement" of the Council of Writing Program Administrators makes a strong case for cumulative, multistage planning/writing/revising as essential for novice learner/writers. This statement maintains that students should

- understand a writing assignment as a series of tasks, including finding, evaluating, analyzing, and synthesizing appropriate primary and secondary sources;
- [use] multiple drafts to create and complete a successful text;
- understand writing as an open process [for] later invention and re-thinking. (324)

These patterns are implemented in the course structures outlined in chapter 5.

Priority Two

Establish expectations and tasks that make writing an intersubjective process of recognizing and responding to others' views and voices.
Evidence from this and other studies shows that such participation helps students recognize knowledge-making as a shared, interactive enterprise and develop a sense of agency in knowledge communities. These outcomes can help students learn the freedoms and responsibilities of long-term, self-directed knowledge-building. Nurturing students' attainment of autonomy will

- help students gain the sense of being insiders in specific knowledge fields;
- help students recognize that writing and knowledge-making are inherently social and interactive;
- strengthen students' understanding of the power and responsibility inherent in specific knowledge-field participation.

These outcomes can help students become wary of easy solutions, more tolerant of complexity, and more willing to criticize and rethink the given. This priority is implemented in the course structures outlined in chapter 5.

Priority Three

Affirm the importance of sustained, cumulative rethinking, reflection, and reformulation for students learning to write as knowledge-makers.
This is a core priority for undergraduate learning. Though revision-based pedagogy has long been a crucial element of composition courses, nevertheless recursive, cumulative learning/writing practices are difficult for American students to acquire—and difficult, as well, for teachers to nurture. Such practices do not take shape easily in the American semester environment. One reason for this is the deadline

pressures of the American semester. Another is the curricular imperative of general education, requiring a range of course experiences at
introductory levels where topic and issue coverage are the dominant
intentions. Only teachers, through course structure and management,
can help undergraduates build the reflective, recursive planning/writ-
ing roles characteristic of experienced knowledge-makers.

This challenge is difficult for undergraduate teachers to implement
in the face of semester pressures. With frequent on-time text-production tasks—short papers, quizzes, exams— built into most American
undergraduate courses, where and how can systemic motives for recursive behavior be constructed? Students will develop recursiveness
in thinking and writing only in response to broad-based expectations
embedded in tasks and courses. These must be constructed to enable
sustained, repeated processes of what Flower terms "appropriation,
co-option, cooperation, or resistance" as students make and remake
meaning during a semester's time (*Construction* 106). Both course and
broader institutional structures must be developed to change American
students' deadline-driven preference for short-burst writing. Course
structures must be devised with time patterns that combine expectations for sustained rethinking with self-directed freedom in recursive
activity. Early, open formulations of ideas and claims about specific
topics will be subject to significant reformulation in final outcomes.

In the next chapter, these guidelines are embodied in specific planning goals for teachers and illustrated in specific course examples.

5 / Teaching Transformative Writing

Teachers' Planning Goals

In chapter 4, I proposed that students be challenged to write transformatively as knowledge-makers in extended, goal-driven writing projects. In this chapter, I describe the pedagogical strategies and course structures that can maximize students' opportunities to write transformatively in extended, self-directed settings.

Opportunities to develop roles as transformative writers in extended writing projects are not readily available to early-semester American undergraduates. To change this traditional pattern of deferral, I propose that undergraduates be challenged to write in goal-driven, self-directed projects in as many different areas as possible from the outset of their studies. As Wallace and Ewald suggest, "Students are in some measure immediately qualified to enter disciplinary debates and to assume authority in constructing disciplinary knowledge" (133). Teachers are key to this process by challenging students to practice self-directed learning and writing in as wide a variety of knowledge settings as possible.

Perhaps the biggest challenge for inexperienced academic writers is to learn the responsible use of freedom. Yet freedom is risky for students and teachers. It may frustrate students accustomed to carrying out explicit instructions about identifying topics for study, methods of inquiry, and text conditions like length and deadline. It may frustrate teachers who want to make sure students fulfill a semester's requirements as well as possible. But the freedom to reconsider intentions, change goals, revise plans, and rework texts is an essential part of productive knowledge work, even though students may well hesitate, become confused, or remain indecisive as projects unfold.

All students in postsecondary environments face this challenge at some point. Yet it is particularly hard for American undergraduate teachers to give open-ended freedom to students tracked by credit/grade point accounting and multiple in-semester assessments in their courses. These pressures are naturalized within the American postsecondary system to such an extent that they feel normal to students and teachers alike. In this environment, failure to complete a term paper by the deadline can do mortal damage to a student's grade. For this reason, it is important to be clear about the consequences of these pressures. Students may see little opportunity to develop the long-term patience and persistence required by the feedback/rethinking/revision process inherent in recursive processes. Because of semester delivery deadlines, they may be unable to make use of a changing or late-developing understanding of issues as they write their term papers. They may also learn—like the students in this study—to be risk-averse as they recognize the constant danger of delay and failure embedded in all recursive practices. The evidence in earlier chapters suggests that these pressures can encourage students to formulate narrow learning/writing goals, trim plans as deadlines draw near, and practice efficient, on-time text production as the safest strategy for success.

While these pressures seem routine to American students and teachers, they block the sort of freedom and self-direction conferred on German students as they choose how, when, where, or even whether to complete a seminar project. In this sense, while it has its drawbacks, the German system better tolerates the extended decision-making and openness to change needed for self-directed writing and knowledge-making. The American semester system does not easily tolerate this flexibility. Thus when American students develop and complete substantive, long-term projects, time must be given to them to develop, make mistakes, rethink, and revise their tasks and texts—a process that often takes experienced writers months or years to carry out. The challenge for American teachers is to construct the appropriate blend of freedom and opportunity for students within the systemic limits of a semester. The following planning goals suggest strategies by which teachers can create such opportunities.

Teachers' Planning Goal One

Undergraduate courses emphasizing transformative writing should be centered on self-directed, goal-driven projects structured to allow multiple opportunities for reflection, rethinking, and revision. Course tasks should be paced so that a semester's duration appears to be a long-term, opportunity-rich horizon for each student. Cumulative semester projects are the best vehicle for immersing students in the processes of topic formation, research, reflection, and writing. Students' freedom to change, shift focus, or reformulate goals is limited by the pressure for closure—projects must conclude, papers must be finished, grades must be given. For these reasons, the inescapable tensions between individual freedom and systemic constraints must be incorporated in course structures themselves. On the one hand, the activities of topic-formation, planning, reformulating, drafting, and revising should appear to students as predictable, time-sensitive stages of task development. But at the same time, these activities should be framed as self-directed, goal-driven choices, open to change and reformulation. Helping students negotiate these ambivalent conditions is an important challenge for teachers as they plan and teach such a course.

Students' ongoing evaluation of their goals and progress is crucial to their success as transformative writers. Invitations for continuous self-monitoring must be built into course structures and teacher expectations. They must be free to reformulate goals, adapt inquiry strategies as appropriate, and sustain progress in a timely fashion. Developing reflectiveness in thinking and writing has been well elaborated, for example, by Flower and Yancey. Both define reflectiveness as a dialectical process of retrospection and interaction with others. Reflectiveness, says Flower, means "build[ing] awareness by 'taking thought' of one's own thinking" (*Construction* 225). As students struggle to synthesize new concepts and information, they undertake "a process of *re-construction* in which meaning emerges from a dialectic between the writer's existing schemas and understanding, her or his performance, and the responses to that performance" (265).

Flower's dialectic brings retrospection, interaction, feedback, and textual revision in a sustained interactive cycle. While sharing Flower's emphasis on dialectical interaction, Yancey also emphasizes the evolution of students' goals: reflection is "the dialectical process by which we develop and achieve, first, specific goals for learning; second, strategies for reaching those goals; and third, the means of whether or not we have met those goals" (6). In basing her model of reflection on persistent goal-evaluation, Yancey says that

> through reflection, we can circle back, return to earlier notes, to earlier understandings and observations, to re-think them. . . . Reflection asks that we explain to others . . . so that *in explaining to others, we explain to ourselves.* We begin to re-understand. (24; original emphasis)

Both models require that teachers build a sequence of opportunities for choice and change into their courses.

Reflective opportunities may be embedded in many different events that lead to a cumulative final text or portfolio. In the course model I outline below, a "checkpoint" for inviting reflection is established for each phase of the course. Grading—a fundamental force in the American undergraduate system—must be carefully planned. Institutional pressures often demand insistent monitoring through quizzes, tests, and short writings, obliging students to attune themselves to continuous grade point calculations. But frequent grading and assessment remind students of their probationary status and diminish their sense of self-directedness as writers and knowledge-makers. In-semester grading should be limited to specific tasks not part of the project development process, such as reading analyses, interpretations, and position papers. Activities such as work plans, journaling, and progress reports should not be graded.

Teachers' Planning Goal Two

In their writing projects, students should take on roles as writers in specific knowledge communities, constituted through classroom and group interactions and grounded in the discursive activities of those knowledge communities. This goal asserts the importance of constructing a classroom as a knowledge community. As I suggested in chapter 4, a knowledge community in an undergraduate setting will be both a material place and a discursive space. Students' interactions will occur in classrooms, offices, cafeteria tables, on-line discussion spaces, and the discursive spaces of course readings, teachers' instructions and lectures, and peers' texts. Students' roles in these spaces will demand constructive interaction, response, and feedback. To achieve this goal, teachers need to ensure that students recognize and understand the roles they are invited to play. Students should be reflexively aware of the roles they play as participants and that these roles carry responsibilities for others' success as well as their own. They should be reminded that they are being asked, not to close off existing personal literacies, but to add new ones that augment their range. Teachers might find the theater metaphor effective in this context. Students must "read for" their new roles—some parts must be learned exactly (citation rules), while other parts have to be developed or (to alter Bartholomae's term) reinvented or even improvised—in the context of the activity. The metaphor of conversation is also suggestive, since talking, reading, and writing are equally important elements of knowledge community activity. All these activities should flow together as students "dispute particulars, redefine issues, add new material, or shift the discussion" (Bazerman 49). As novices in knowledge communities, students will often be reluctant to articulate ideas they are unsure of or to attempt new textual strategies. They need to be reminded that uncertainty is essential to writing as knowledge makers. By devising repeated opportunities for reflexive participation, teachers can help students learn to be patient with their own inexperience.

Teachers' Planning Goal Three

Students should be expected to learn rhetorical and stylistic strategies that use the discursive conventions of the topic field and reflect the intersubjective basis of knowledge construction.

Students may fear the complex reading and writing demands of specific field-related genres. But if undergraduates are to write as knowledge-makers, they must learn the rhetorical nature of authorship in knowledge communities and the discursive strategies practiced in these communities. They must discover that, as Geisler says, texts are written as "acts that can be understood only within a temporal and interpersonal framework" and that "people write texts not simply to say things but to do things: to persuade, to argue, to excuse" (87). The undergraduates in Geisler's study gave little attention to "rhetorical process" issues as they wrote and did not emphasize the interplay of contested views as they shaped their own opinions (225). In another study of undergraduates in introductory courses, McCarthy and Fishman describe the "boundary conversations" that take place as students "step gradually into the unfamiliar [disciplinary] neighborhood, at first listening closely, then perhaps deciding to try some phrases of the new language . . . and trying out new roles" (422). They develop "new sorts of listening" and learn to "juxtapose conflicting ways of knowing" as they discover the knowledge patterns of their disciplines (465). As both Geisler and McCarthy and Fishman demonstrate, this transition requires continuous repositioning into new, more complex rhetorical relationships as students develop authorship in a specific knowledge area.

Students may resist these goals. They may avoid using field-specific terms in their writing, misuse them, or, as first-year political science student Jana does in her proseminar paper (see chapter 3), reproduce them accurately but neutrally, without a personal voice to interpret or negotiate competing positions. Since strategies of analysis, interpretation, and argument differ widely among disciplines, there is no master formula for helping students integrate these strategies into their writing. Teachers must be willing to explain why a field-specific term is better than a general or common term for a particular rhetorical purpose. They must tolerate inexperienced attempts to build connections between personal language and special discourses and find chances to show students where they can adapt their language to the topic field. It is important to remember that, as chapter 4 suggests, students' personal voices should remain the core of this transitional process—the reflective center from which multiple other voices and ideas can be negotiated.

Building Project-Based Courses

Course models emphasizing extended writing projects have been proposed in various curricular contexts. Some have roots in writing-intensive and writing-across-the-curriculum initiatives, while others emerge from the long tradition of research writing in composition courses. David A. Joliffe, for example, proposes a pattern that begins with an "inquiry contract" requiring students to articulate learning/writing goals early in the semester and then develop a series of activities shaping the students' understanding of the topic in relation to "what *other people* feel, think, believe, and know about your subject" (*Inquiry* 72; original emphasis). After writing a series of journaling tasks, reading responses, "informative reports," and "exploratory essays" during the semester, students compose a "working documents project designed to change people's minds" as a final text (4). In this model, the emphasis is on students' discovery of the knowledge-making required to write persuasively for others in the final text of the project.

Another model emphasizing an essayist approach to research/writing tasks is offered by Ballenger, who maintains that to encourage "the genuine spirit of inquiry" for students, "questions that research can help answer" should be a primary planning target for teachers as they develop extended writing tasks (16). He argues that the "researched *essay*, not the research paper," is the best way to ensure that students are "jolted out of a passive role and become much more active agents in the negotiation about what might be true" (106). He emphasizes the value of "narrative notetaking"—reflective, expanded note entries—to help students "struggle to take possession of other peoples' words" as they develop their inquiries (109). These entries, suggests Ballenger, will enable students to engage with others' voices as they articulate their own views of contested issues.

A broad range of project types are described by Davis and Shadle, who emphasize "the experiential excitement of not knowing" as a spur for students' readiness to explore topics through "a variety of modes, genres . . . and media" (430). While they value the "personal research paper" and the "research essay" as occasions for students' entering "current debates" and "inscribing personal issues" in their learning, they propose a "multi-genre/media research project" as a stronger alternative model for students' projects. A multigenre project may "suspend and/or decenter the master consciousness . . . inscribed in the essay" and bring out instead "a wandering consciousness" that may result in "threads left hanging, [or] questions remaining" (431).

The project-based proposal I outline below shares the emphasis on reflectiveness found in these models. In addition, it foregrounds three other significant features:

- students' sustained self-direction throughout the project
- students' articulation of their roles as writers and knowl-edge-makers
- students' immersion in the relational, intersubjective activi-ties of knowledge construction

Project-Based Courses: A Model

A semester project should consist of a sequence of writings—jour-naling, analyses, interpretations, position papers, progress reports—focused on a specific topic and culminating in the production of a significant final text or text/media combination. Project presenta-tion/discussions by each student may accompany the production of the final text.

To maximize opportunities for long-term rethinking and revision, course structures should

- require students to establish a project focus early in the semester;
- offer a process of project development open to global change in thinking and text planning;
- schedule specific opportunities for reformulation, restate-ment, and change as students' projects evolve.

Negotiating their own project goals will jump-start students' thinking about their intentions in the course and invite them to see that rethinking and rewriting are not simply wheel-spinning but the means by which project goals are kept in sight. Contingency must be built into the project development process. Students may discover that they want to change focus or develop a more workable topic. They may discover that they cannot complete resource searches or field research because sources are not available or simply because they waited too long. Courses must be structured to identify and deal with these contingencies.

The phases in the structural outline below are centered on a cumulative, semester-long project. Though the phases are laid out in a sequence here, they will overlap and interconnect as students make progress in their projects. The outline suggests a number of "checkpoints" at which students may reflect and assess progress, orally and in writing, in conferences with the instructor and in peer-group discussions. In the first phase, the work plan allows students to articulate goals and form plans to achieve those goals. In the second phase, instructor-student conferences give students opportunities to discuss progress in locating resources, researching, and turning up connections between concepts and applications as work gets underway. The progress report in the third phase is a significant checkpoint for global reflection on the status of the project. It enables students to ask themselves whether they have located enough resources for their original goals, to clarify what difficulties they are having, and to identify major issues and controversies. The fourth phase includes several weeks of drafting and revision, including peer and instructor feedback, to help students shape final texts.

MODEL COURSE OUTLINE

PHASE ONE   TASKS
- Define issues and problems.
- Form project goals and strategies.
- Participate in interactive classroom feedback and response.
- Negotiate project plan with instructor.

ACTIVITIES

- Begin readings and discussions.
- Develop work plans and inquiry strategies.
- Consult with instructor concerning project plan.

*Checkpoint.

PHASE TWO   TASKS

- Read; discuss course readings.
- Write analyses, interpretations, position papers, reports, journal notes.
- Begin project research—locate and acquire library and archival field resources; identify/interview respondents.
- Engage in classroom and peer-group feedback and response.

ACTIVITIES

- Identify strategies for primary text analysis.
- Search resources in libraries, archives, records, and Internet; conduct interviews and transcribe them.
- Read and write analyses, interpretations, and position papers; write in journal.
- Discuss research processes, early findings or contested issues in peer groups.

*Checkpoint.

PHASE THREE   TASKS

- Read and discuss course materials including "finding, evaluating, analyzing, and synthesizing appropriate primary and secondary sources" (Council).
- Write analyses, interpretations, position papers, reports, and journal notes.
- Continue project research—locate and acquire library, archival, Internet, and field resources; conduct field research.

- Develop progress report.
- Consult with instructor about progress report.

ACTIVITIES
- Analyze materials for contested issues or points of conflict.
- Reflect on/think through journaling and group/classroom discussions.
- Read and write analyses, interpretations, and position papers.
- Receive peer-group feedback and responses.

*Checkpoint.
- Consult with instructor about progress issues.

*Checkpoint.

PHASE FOUR TASKS
- Rethink and reformulate concepts and conclusions.
- Organize, draft, and revise final text.
- Solicit small-group workshop/instructor feedback.
- Make project presentation.

ACTIVITIES
- Draft and revise final text/media/portfolio.
- Give and receive feedback about revisions in peer-group workshop.

*Checkpoint.
- Receive feedback from instructor at student's request.

*Checkpoint.
- Make group or individual presentation of project.

Project-Based Courses: Two Examples

In the following sections, two courses featuring self-directed, goal-driven writing projects are described, including course goals, tasks, student texts, and my responses to them. I taught each of these courses recently as part of the curriculum of the English department of Midwestern University. The first is a first-year seminar featuring students' research projects focused on their families' literacy histories, requiring readings in literacy theory and narratives and culminating in an extended report. The second is an upper-level literature course focused on the work of Oscar Wilde, drawing students from a variety of disciplines within the university. I asked students to read Wilde's work in light of various cultural representations of Wilde's public persona and write an extended interpretive study.

First-Year Seminar: Exploring Literacy—Ours and Others'

Student project: Ann explores her family literacy history

This course was created as a first-year seminar. Such seminars are one-semester courses on a variety of topics; all entering freshmen must choose one. They are intended, in the words of the university catalog, to "create community among entering students," integrate them "into an academic culture," enhance "writing and verbal communication skills," and focus on "ways of knowing." The class included students from the arts and sciences, business, journalism, education, and pharmacy colleges of the university. The course began with an assignment to define the term "literacy" as students currently understood it. Students read and analyzed theory-based literacy studies as well as literacy narratives, including Victoria Purcell-Gates's *Other Peoples' Words*. At the same time, they did ongoing research into their literacy projects. The goal of the seminar was to help students learn about literacy issues and basic techniques of literacy research; research their personal, family, and community literacy contexts; and then construct a literacy history of family members or a family group.

During the course, there were multiple opportunities for rethinking, review, and reformulation of viewpoints. The final paper—a theory-responsive, research-based literacy narrative—gave students opportunities to reformulate initial understandings of literacy issues, compare and evaluate divergent theoretical positions, and construct a personal perspective on literacy project. Students were asked to integrate their data and findings into broader issues of literacy study, using field-specific terms where needed.

Ann, whose work exemplifies one student's progress through the course, was a first-year student from a midwestern state. She was enrolled in the College of Education and was thinking about majoring in English as her disciplinary specialty. She chose to write a family literacy history, focused on the literacy stories of her grandmothers and her parents.

Exploring Literacies—Ours and Others'
Reading List
> Garnes, *Writing Lives*
> Purcell-Gates, *Other Peoples' Words*
> Course readings included articles by Auerbach, Brandt, Goodman, and others

Phase One: Defining Terms, Setting Goals, Planning Tasks
Weeks 1–4

In the first weeks, students begin exploring literacy issues and research and thinking about their personal literacies and literacy contexts.

COURSE TASKS
- Explore project topics—"what do I want to focus on?"
- Read/discuss (concepts, analyses, applications).
- Discuss strategies for issue/concept analyses.
- Develop work plan and inquiry strategies for project.
- Consult with instructor about work plan.

PROJECT ACTIVITIES
- Write initial topic definition (first week).
- Hold initial planning conferences with instructor (third and fourth weeks).
- Write draft of work plan for term project, including goals and inquiry strategies (fourth week).

• Meet with instructor about work plan.

(See Ann's initial topic definition and my response below.)

Phase Two: Inquiry Processes: Researching, Accumulating, Synthesizing
Weeks 5–7

In the second phase, students begin researching oral and written sources, accumulating data for their literacy projects. They also continue reading and discussing literacy narratives and studies, meeting in peer-group workshops, and writing analyses.

COURSE TASKS
• Research library sources.
• Read/discuss (concepts, analyses, applications).
• Write analyses of literacy studies and narratives.
• Work in peer groups.

PROJECT ACTIVITIES
• Begin researching project-related written and oral sources (see appendix 5.1).
• Locate literacy respondents; plan and carry out interviews.

OTHER COURSE ACTIVITIES
• Write/discuss analyses of course readings.
• Discuss task progress in peer-group workshops.

(See Ann's reading analysis and my response below.)

Phase Three: Assimilating, Synthesizing, Reflecting, Reporting
Weeks 8–12

In the third phase, students continue accumulating data from written and oral sources and write a progress report on current research findings. They continue reading and discussing literacy narratives and research studies, write another reading analysis, then write a progress report identifying connections between literacy readings and emerging findings of their literacy projects, outlining issues to be developed further in final draft.

COURSE TASKS

- Continue interviews, accumulate interview data, and transcribe and analyze transcripts for data patterns.
- Analyze source materials for dominant issues or points of contention.
- Read/discuss (concepts, analyses, applications).
- Develop progress report.

PROJECT ACTIVITIES

- Continue interviewing, transcribe interviews, and analyze data.
- Write/present progress reports on emerging project findings and connections with theories and issues in readings. Not graded.
- Consult with instructor on project progress.

OTHER COURSE ACTIVITIES:

- Write/discuss analyses of course readings.
- Discuss task progress in peer-group workshops.

(See Ann's progress report and my response below.)

Phase Four: Text Organizing, Drafting, Revision; Project Presentations
Weeks 12–16

In the fourth phase, students complete analyses of literacy information from interview transcripts, formulate connections between literacy patterns and theory issues, and organize, draft, and present text of final project.

COURSE TASKS

- Analyze data in relation to literacy theory issues; develop project conclusions.

- Draft/revise project papers (weeks 11–15).
- Prepare and give project presentations.

PROJECT ACTIVITIES
- Make final synthesis of informant data.
- Draft/revise project text.
- Present term project report for class discussion (weeks 12–14).
- Submit final draft of term paper at course conclusion, after project presentations.

(See parts of Ann's final text and my comments below.)

Ann's topic definition

Task. Describe meanings of "literacy" as you understand it; note areas you are most unsure of; outline briefly what you would like to learn about literacy in relation to personal and family literacy histories.

Ann's initial topic definition and project plan. The dictionary defines literacy as "the condition of being able to read and write." Reading and writing play a major role in the lives of everyone on a daily basis. I have heard the term literacy used most often with literacy rates by country, etc. Hearing low literacy rates in other countries makes me realize how lucky I am to know how to read and write. Besides this, I don't know much about literacy research or how people do it. I know I have had a good school education and I feel I have developed good literacy levels myself, and my parents have encouraged me to read from an early age, which is good to build on for later life. Since one main goal in this course is to look into my family background for their literacy history, I would like to look at my grandparents' religious and national backgrounds. One grandmother came from an eastern European country and it would be interesting to see how she learned her English while living as a farm wife. My other grandmother was also a farm wife from a very Catholic family. From my grandmas to my parents and on down to me, literacy seemed to come naturally with no problems. Maybe I could find out something about why this would be.

My response to Ann. Ann, I like the way you describe your own advantages in school and home as you learned to read and write. Your interest in your family's diverse cultural background will be a good focus for your literacy project. You are so lucky to have your parents and grandparents all available to tell you about their literacy backgrounds! You have a wonderful opportunity to do some first-hand research by interviewing them and seeing how their histories come together in your family network. You'll find some of our readings in this course directly relate to issues of family literacy study. I look forward to talking with you about this.

Following my written response, we talked in our first conference about the human and methodological aspects of data-gathering. I saw my main task as helping Ann take on the role of field researcher as she carried out her interviewing tasks. I asked her to review what she knew of her family's general history in preparation and suggested ways she could help her parents and grandmothers be comfortable in a formal interview setting. We identified a set of questions for her interviews (based on a format we had discussed in class), and I asked her to draw up a specific interview schedule to assure getting her data on a timely basis.

Ann's second reading analysis

Task. In this assignment, the task is to analyze an assertion or claim that appears to be similar in two different readings. Consider the following questions: What do these ideas seem to have in common? How might they differ? Also, talk a bit about how this idea or claim affects your understanding of your project's research goal.

Ann's text: "Literacy in Different Cultures." According to the philosopher Aristotle, "What we learn to do we learn by doing." In Elsa Robert Auerbach's piece "Toward a Social-Contextual Approach to Family Literacy" she shows that she would agree with this statement, at least in regards to literacy. Auerbach has come up with a model which she believes supports the most successful approach to literacy. Her model is very important in the story of Jenny and her son Donny as Urban Appalachians living in a ghetto in some major city within the United States. Both of them are illiterate. Their story is told in Victoria Purcell-Gates' book *Other People's Words,* which documents their experiences while receiving literacy tutoring and dealing with the difference between their culture and what is otherwise known as the "mainstream culture" (Auerbach 173). Jenny and Donny's case greatly supports Auerbach's claims, showing that her ideas are accurate.

[In this paragraph Ann describes Auerbach's critique of the idea that "non-mainstream families" cannot provide literacy environments. Ann says that Jenny and Donny's "environments are not lacking, they are simply just different." Ann exemplifies Auerbach's "difference" thesis by describing an episode from Purcell-Gates's story about young Donny, who receives pencils from the teacher and, because "the need for pencils was almost nonexistent for their family," uses the pencils for toy fishing poles. "In other words," says Ann, "he took the tutor's attempts to inject her 'cultural tools of literacy' (Purcell-Gates 153) into his world, and turned them into concepts that he already knew about within his own culture."]

[In this paragraph Ann discusses Auerbach's thesis that "home experiences" strongly shape a child's literacy experiences. Ann describes the child Donny's failure to learn to read or write as stemming from his parents' refusal to "do literacy" with their children. In support of her point, Ann cites Auerbach's claim that parents often "avoid replicating what they remembered as negative experiences (Auerbach 173)." "Their bad memories of school," concludes Ann, "allowed Jenny and her husband to keep many literate interactions from evolving into a part of their everyday life."]

Literacy is something that usually must begin in the home. However, in some cases that is not possible. For these people, because of their background, including their cultural ties which caused them to value certain aspects of life over others, it is just not an acceptable request. With the contention that our society has today that "illiteracy breeds illiteracy" (Auerbach 167), we make it almost impossible for cultures other than the "mainstream" to succeed. For a country promoting equal opportunity this simply seems hypocritical. Literacy should be something all families from different cultures can develop.

I have found some interesting examples of the connections between home and school literacy in my own research, because my mother and grandmother were not mainstream in their backgrounds. But they both learned to be literate because of their strong family cultures.

My response to Ann. I really like the way you use Auerbach's ideas to interpret the impact of home and family cultures on schooled literacy and to interpret some features of Donny and Jenny's situation. When you apply Auerbach's idea of people avoiding negative school experiences to Donny and Jenny's case, it helped me understand why Donny's parents would resist the attempts made by his schoolteacher to get them to help him learn to read. You use the interplay between these two readings well to demonstrate how schooled literacies may be disconnected from personal and home literacy situations. When you prepare your progress report, I would like you to explore how Auerbach's insights, and the family-school connections Purcell-Gates writes about, might give you some perspective on your own family literacy history. Let's talk about this more in our conference.

My interpretation of Ann's analysis. In this analysis, the second in the course, written in week 7, Ann brings together two readings—one theoretical and one narrative—that describe conflicts between home and schooled literacy. Her progress in building a role as a writer in the field of literacy studies is shown in two ways. First, she shows that she has learned how to read specific cases in terms of a theoretical approach, as she applies insights from the Auerbach article, focusing on home-school relations, to Purcell-Gates's narrative of an Appalachian family. Second, her use of Auerbach's words shows her efforts to assimilate the terms and usages of literacy study. Some terms she has appropriated into her own lexicon ("oral interaction," "literate interaction," "literacy situation"), while others she uses only within quotes ("'mainstream'" and "'non-mainstream,'" "'culturally legitimate,'" "'uses of literacy'") to suggest her reliance on viewpoints (Auerbach's and Purcell-Gates's) she sees as outside her own range of authority. The fact that she carefully distinguishes between these levels of textual authority shows an awareness of her novice status as a literacy researcher. And she has maintained a clear personal voice in negotiating these levels of authority.

Ann's progress report (week 8)

Task. The progress report should respond to these questions:

- What is my progress to date?
- Have I located enough resources to provide the background, data, readings, and range of competing views needed to achieve my original goals?
- Must my project goals be reassessed in light of my current research progress? If so, how?
- How would I describe the roles I am taking on as I develop my project, and what do these roles require?
- What major issues, conflicts, or controversies have emerged from my research and study so far? Do they differ from what I expected? How do I think they might shape my conclusions?

> *Ann's progress report.* I am finding that there is by no means a single meaning of the term literacy. In my own research I am finding both sides of the issue, that living at home teaches you literacy, like reading the Bible, also other situations show home reading and school teaching seem to work together.

In my research I am exploring the literacy worlds of four of my family members, which include my mom, my mom's mom, my dad, and my dad's mom. My dad and I both grew up in the same small town in Iowa. We both had the same teacher who was a literacy mentor as described by Deborah Brandt. Neither dad nor I will forget her in our literacy development. We also had a "reading corner" where we went to read by ourselves, we both had the same ideas that way.

[In this section Ann outlines both grandmothers' cultural origins and main literacy stages. Her paternal grandmother "went to a Lutheran church school, and learned her literacy from the Bible." Her "mom's mother" had a farming background and a Bible-based literacy development. Ann concludes that both "show Deborah Brandt's description of Bible texts in a religious family culture."]

As far as my roles, looking at my family's stories really makes me look at who I am and how literacy has played a role in where I've ended up. I think in my paper I want to explore the religious connections in my grandmas' literacy histories, and I want to deal with the issue of school and home literacy connections that I have found. Then I will try to show how these literacy stories related to the theories and other stories we have discussed.

My response to Ann. Ann, I really like the direction you're going in here. You are doing a good job of combining the roles of literacy researcher and interpretive historian as you describe your main findings about your grandparents' literacy backgrounds. I think you describe a picture that, overall, sounds like a story of diverse origins that adapted to the literacy contexts of the Midwest. But also, it doesn't seem like you are saying that either grandma was part of any "melting pot," because each was somewhat outside the mainstream culture, as you say. So I am hoping as you write your paper you will help me understand how Bible readings and religious traditions (like Catholicism) might have come together into your family's tradition. Also, it's really interesting about your dad's love for a reading corner just like yours!

I'd like you to connect some of these points with issues we've explored in our readings. How do you see the "reading corner" issue fitting in with Auerbach's discussion of home literacy as a means of reinforcing school literacy? You also suggest that Brandt's "literacy sponsor" idea helps account for the teacher's influence on both you and your dad. I think that's really an interesting point, and I'd like to know more about how this teacher connected so strongly with both you and your dad. It would be very helpful to develop these issues as you write.

My interpretation of Ann's progress report. Ann was still elaborating various meanings of literacy while accumulating information about her family's literacy histories. She already sensed the overall shape of her narrative but wasn't sure how to analyze its salient points. Although she recognized that both grandmothers shared religious influences, she didn't think those influences formed a "melting pot," since both grandmothers stayed close to their religious and cultural origins. She also wasn't sure how she could connect these religious traditions with the "literacy sponsor" model. In addition, Ann was trying to understand the dialectic between home and school literacy environments that Auerbach describes. Overall, she was juggling complex and somewhat contradictory variables, since religion had both positive and negative impacts on her family's literacies.

This literacy-history project poses a significant challenge to first-year students, because it requires them to integrate two genres—literacy-acquisition theory and literacy field research. I wanted to help Ann recognize the differing effects of Bible reading and Catholic schooling in her grandmothers' histories. I wasn't sure how clearly Ann would be able to sort out these issues in her final draft, but I wanted her to try. I also wanted her to explore how her grandmothers' literacy successes influenced her parents' development and her own home environment, using the "reading corner" story as a case in point. Finally, I wanted to encourage her to reflect on the relationship between home and school literacies in both grandmothers' situations.

Family or community group literacy study

Task. This project asks you to research a family or community group literacy history and write a literacy narrative based on this research. As you plan and prepare for this project, you will be working in the role of literacy researchers, learning how those who do literacy studies think and write in their fields. You will be asked to select some participants, interview them, transcribe these interviews, and use this data in developing your literacy narrative. We will prepare for this project through readings, discussions, and conferences. All of us in class will act as resources and feedback-givers for each other during the project. As part of your planning, you will need to prepare specific questions to ask during your interviews. You will also need a recorder to tape the interviews.

Ann's literacy study: "A Look into My Family Literacy History." Literacy learning is different for people in every part of the world. Different cultures, beliefs and time periods are what bring about this variety. I've taken the time to explore the literacy world of four of my family members, including my mom, my mom's mom, my dad, and my dad's mom. Each of these people grew up in a different learning environment that helped shape their understanding of literacy today, and these are their stories.

My dad grew up in a small town in Iowa. From the time he was born until the time he moved away to go to college, he lived in the same house and attended the same school district for his entire life. Dad learned to read and write from many teachers along the way. He told me, "Mom and dad knew the importance of having a good reading background, a good 'literacy background' as you are calling it. They always made me do my homework before I was ever allowed to go out and play." His "literacy sponsor," as Deborah Brandt calls it, was his 7th grade writing teacher. He told me, "she would spend so much time with me, helping me through a couple novels that I was having problems with. I always looked up to her, and I knew she was someone I would always remember."

Amazingly, looking at my own literacy learning, I too had a literacy mentor—the very same person who helped my dad in his literacy development. When I had her she was my home room instructor, an elderly lady, but that simply made her more approachable. Her influence on both of us is an example of Brandt's idea of a literacy "sponsor" who motivated us to learn to read and write. She also is a positive example of the "transmission of school practices" model that Auerbach criticizes, because in my family's case home and school literacy learning obviously reinforced each other. Our teacher helped my dad read better and she also encouraged me to read in my home, so there was similarity in both environments.

[In this section, Ann describes her own love for reading in the "reading place" she and her dad had in common: "Just like him, I had a place I went to read when it was nice outside, and I called it 'my corner.' (That place, by the way, was outside in a corner where our patio met the deck). Dad and I got a chuckle out of the fact that we both had a 'corner.' I think this reinforces one of Auerbach's statements, that 'parents use and transmit literacy in specific ways that schools expect gives these children an advantage' (168)."]

[In this section Ann describes both grandmothers' histories. Her dad's mother was born in the Ukraine, where her family fled Bolsheviks, deciding "they did not want their children to grow up in this kind of country, so they decided to leave." They settled in Mexico, then relocated in Nebraska where she learned English. Ann quotes her as saying, "It didn't take long. I bet in three weeks we could speak English." She went to a Lutheran church school, "so naturally much of her literacy learning stemmed from the readings of the Bible." Ann's maternal grandmother was also raised in a rural midwestern environment. She "lived on a small farm in the outskirts of a tiny town in Iowa, and was raised under strict Catholic parents," says Ann, quoting her grandmother as saying, "You know, most of my literacy learning stemmed from our learning of the Bible. We would read stories and learn meanings of words that we did not know."]

Four separate people, four separate places, and four separate stories. Yet somehow, they all seem to be related. And the largest theme throughout all of their stories goes back to religion. Both families show the influence of religious reading as Brandt describes it in her article "Remembering Reading," where she says that "reading religious materials was part of a family routine or holiday ritual" (462). In all of their literacy learning, one book that everyone remembered and mentioned at some point was the Bible. However, my mom wanted her kids to be able to think for themselves, and didn't necessarily believe the "rules" of the Catholic religion. And it's because of these feelings that she would not let her children go to a Catholic school system. So both grandmothers had a strong religious influence in their literacy development, but it didn't carry into my mom's generation. For them reading the Bible was important, so home reading and school teaching seem to work together.

You have just heard the literacy histories of four of my family members. It is quite a perspective, looking at how I've come to be here in the middle of Iowa and how literacy has played a role in where I've ended up. I have found out a little bit of what it is like to study literacy in families in this project, and to connect their literacy with some ideas that full-time researchers have found in many other literacy situations. What's more is that my literacy learning is just beginning. I'm only a fifth of the way done with my life, so maybe someday I will have a very interesting literacy story to tell to my grandchild. I can only hope so.

My interpretation of Ann's final draft. Ann did well in developing her roles as literacy researcher and historian, with a solid effort at framing findings by means of useful theoretical perspectives drawn from Brandt, Auerbach, and Purcell-Gates. She made good use of quotes from her interviews and offered a nice synoptic perspective in her concluding paragraph, demonstrating her control of the narrative frame. She used Brandt's "literacy sponsor" motif to clarify the strong teacher element she shared with her dad, and she applied Auerbach's discussion of home/school literacies to clarify the complex influences of religion in her family and to explain the "reading corner" tradition. Overall, I think her work showed positive transformative features, including applying theoretical perspectives to specific case situations, building a strong authorial voice, and shaping her own perspective on her family's complex literacy histories. At the same time, her inexperience as a novice participant in literacy study was reflected in a couple of ways. She perceived theory largely as support for her own findings and did not use the conflicting aspects of religious influence in her family to test the adequacy of Auerbach's formulation of home/school literacy connections. She did not enter what Geisler terms the "rhetorical problem space" of her topic, using her findings to probe relations among theories and theorists—showing, for example, that some of Brandt's statements run counter to some of Auerbach's. She did maintain a strong personal voice as she integrated the elements of her narrative history, and I thought that was a good achievement for a first-year student.

Upper-Level Literature Course: Oscar Wilde: Life as Theater
Student project: Scott explores the meanings
of transgression in Wilde's Salome

This course was designed as part of the English department's upper-level literature offerings. However, these courses are open to a general clientele within the university, and the twenty-five students in this class ranged from sophomores to seniors from arts and sciences, journalism, education, and even pharmacy. A minority were English majors, so no general assumptions could be made about students' backgrounds in literary interpretation. During the course, students read *The Picture of Dorian Gray,* several plays, and some short fiction, poetry, and prose works, along with short excerpts of cultural texts and representations of Wilde in magazine illustrations, photographs, and caricatures. Discussions focused on Wilde's multiple, ambiguous identities in contemporary cultural, social, and legal contexts.

During the course, there were multiple opportunities for rethinking and reformulation of viewpoints during the semester. The primary writing task was a semester project in which students developed an approach to a work or works of Wilde in relation to specific interpretive perspectives they chose. They were asked to choose their topics and write a work plan to identify the reading and research needed for the project. Other writing tasks included three short papers focused on interpretive or historical/cultural issues related to Wilde's work.

Scott, whose work represents one student's progress through this course, was a senior theater major. He had taken two semesters of theater history and had several acting credits to his name on campus but had little experience in literary interpretation. He was not accustomed to extended writing projects in his major courses, which were oriented toward acting and stagecraft. I chose Scott's work for this course narrative because his efforts to define his roles and authority in the topic field represent the cross-disciplinary challenges often facing American undergraduates.

Oscar Wilde: Life as Theater
Reading List
> Wilde:
> *The Critic as Artist*
> *The Picture of Dorian Gray*
> *Lady Windermere's Fan*
> *The Ideal Husband*
> *The Importance of Being Earnest*
> *De Profundis*
> Assorted poetry, short fiction, letters
> Interpretive essays and chapters by Behrendt, Dollimore, Meyer, and others

Phase One: Defining Terms, Setting Goals, Planning Tasks, Beginning Text Readings/Discussions
Weeks 1–4

COURSE TASKS

- Explore project topic—"what do I want to focus on?" Develop work plans.
- Read/discuss primary texts, interpretive arguments, and contextual materials.

PROJECT ACTIVITIES

- Write initial topic exploration (second week).
- Hold initial planning conference with instructor (third and fourth weeks).
- Write draft of work plan for term project, including goals and inquiry strategies (fourth week).

(See Scott's initial topic definition and my response below.)

Phase Two: Reading, Writing about Assigned Texts, Identifying/Acquiring/Assimilating Project Readings
Weeks 5–8

COURSE TASKS

- Read/discuss primary texts.
- Write interpretive analyses.
- Discuss project issues in peer-group meetings.
- Research textual/visual sources in libraries and on the Internet.
- Journal in response to research readings.
- Discuss research processes, early findings, and contested issues.

PROJECT ACTIVITIES

- Identify, acquire, and read interpretive sources.

- Maintain research journal.

(See examples of Scott's research journal entries and my responses below.)

Weeks 9–12

COURSE TASKS
- Read/discuss primary texts.
- Research project sources in libraries and on the Internet.
- Write/present progress reports on emerging project research, interpretations, and connections with theories and issues in readings. Not graded.

PROJECT ACTIVITIES
- Write and present progress report.
- Meet with instructor (week 10).

(See Scott's progress report and my response below.)

Phase Four: Text Organizing, Drafting, Revision; Project Presentations
Weeks 13–16

COURSE TASKS
- Organize notes, outlines, and drafting.
- Draft and revise final paper.
- Get feedback on draft from peer groups.
- Make presentations of course projects.

PROJECT ACTIVITIES
- Draft and revise final paper.
- Present summary of course project.
- Submit final draft of term paper to instructor at course conclusion, after project presentations.

(See parts of Scott's final paper and my comments below.)

Scott's topic definition

Task. Scott's first task was to develop a proposal for his term project:

> The term project should develop an approach to a work or works of Wilde—fiction, drama, poetry, or prose—in relation to your choice of interpretive perspectives. The primary goal of the project is to shape your own interpretation of Wilde's text(s) in response to views and perspectives you see as relevant to your own interpretive interests. Wilde's work has been very controversial, and one challenge of this project is to construct your approach clearly in relation to competing approaches. Another challenge is for you to reflect, as you develop your project, on the roles you construct for yourself as a reader and interpreter. Developing readings of Wilde's work will probably bring you into the interpretive wars that characterize literary study today—be forewarned! We will explore these controversies together in and out of class, and I look forward to working with you.

Scott's topic proposal. My interest is in the term "transgression" which I hear you use in class, and it seems to mean so many different things. It sounds like it could mean violating some sexual rules in society or maybe something criminal, but I am not sure what at this point. As a theater major I know that lots of playwrights opposed societal norms and showed how social values needed to be changed. I think I would like to study some of Wilde's plays as far as how they represent transgression, so I will try to apply this term to some of his plays. I need to read more of them before I focus my project any further.

My response to Scott. Scott, I think "transgression" is a key term in recent interpretive perspectives on Wilde, and I think you'll find it a good framework for developing some readings of his work. For example, this term leads you straight into "queer theory," versions of which we will discuss in class.

One question related to your interest is how we can read gay or lesbian identity textually. I suggest you look at Moe Meyer's essay in our course readings, as well as Lee Edelman's *Homographesis*, especially the sections where he talks about *The Picture of Dorian Gray* and Wilde's trial (none of this is easy reading—be patient!). Also look at Jonathan Dollimore's book *Sexual Dissidence*, on reserve, which suggests the term "transgressive aesthetic" to describe the relationship between Wilde's artistic goals and his homosexual identity. Another possibility for investigation would be to follow your interest in studying Wilde's plays in relation to the transgression theme. I can suggest a couple of possibilities. One might be to connect transgression with the dandy figure that several interpreters have found significant in his comedies. Another might be to look at his *Salome*, a play drawn from the biblical texts which only got performed in Paris in Wilde's lifetime because it was considered too blatantly sexual for the English stage at the time. It's pretty striking! We'll talk more about these possibilities when we meet.

Scott's topic and work plan resulting from our conferencing. I'd like to focus on the play *Salome*, and develop my interpretations of this play as an example of transgression. In order to get some critical understanding for this project, I will look at some different readings. I will read Powell and Satzinger on the theater environment and dramatic tradition in Wilde's period. I will also look at the writing of Edelman and Meyer to see what ideas about Wilde's image of transgression I can find. I will also analyze the play as a drama, and demonstrate how Wilde structures it for maximum effect as theater. I will try to see how these different approaches can show different sides of the play for readers.

Scott's journal

Week 6 journal entry. I've just finished reading *Salome* and it's quite violent in its imagery, I think. Salome's desire to kiss Iokanaan's lips seems to drive the dramatic energy of the play to its climax, which is pretty shocking. She runs the gamut, from the whiteness of his skin to the darkness of his hair, and then the red of his lips which turns into blood. This combination seems to transgress many social norms, from sexual contact to touching a dead body. So I'm thinking the idea of transgression here is connected with crossing social boundaries, where Wilde wanted to shock the audience, for sure.

My response to Scott's journaling. Scott, I like the way you call attention to the striking imagery of the play and suggest that the force of this imagery might be a kind of transgression itself.

Week 8 journal entry. I've been trying to read Edelman's writing on homosexual identity, where he says this identity can be known and represented as a self-identity. He talks about Dorian Gray discovering himself in the portrait, finding out what he did not recognize before about himself. So I guess this suggests that transgression is somewhat of an issue of how we perceive it, that if we see signs of it, that makes it real for us, like for Dorian Gray. I don't know how this connects with *Salome* though.

My response to Scott's Week 8 journaling. Scott, I'm glad you're working with Edelman, because his theorizing could help you build an interpretation of *Salome* grounded in issues of sexual identity, which you've said is one of your interests. Keep reading!

Scott's progress report

Task. The progress report should respond to these questions:

- What is my progress to date?
- Have I located enough resources to provide the background, data, readings, and range of competing views needed to achieve my original goals?
- Must my project goals be reassessed in light of my current research progress? If so, how?
- How would I describe the roles I am taking on as I develop my project, and what do these roles require?

• What major issues, conflicts, or controversies have emerged from my research and study so far? Do they differ from what I expected? How do I think they might shape my conclusions?

Scott's progress report. I haven't had too much trouble finding the books I wanted. I got the Dollimore book and the Powell book, which gave me some theater history background. I've also got some on-line articles. Another book I found is Ellmann who talks a lot about the biographical background of *Salome,* how it was done in Paris but couldn't be staged in London. Another good book is Powell's book about the milieu for the play. I read some of Edelman's text and Meyer's article. I like the discussions we had about Beardsley's illustrations for the play, because they seem to represent a transgressive attitude about sex. His drawings show transgendered images of girls, which seem to be intended to hit the reader in the eye, maybe transgress against ideas of official "decency" the reader might have. Another kind of transgression comes from an on-line article I read by Tucker, who says that Salome's fate is supposed to show punishment for transgressions against a Catholic moral code. I don't agree with this, maybe because the whole article came from a Catholic website and might be biased.

I am still trying to figure out how to express the ideas of transgression in this play. The imagery in the play shows the white skin and red lips and blood that all pull together and make it seem both violent and sexual at the same time. I think that's one kind of transgression Wilde wants to make, pulling sex and violence together. Wilde's other plays seem to me mostly just good theater with witty dialogue. Only *Salome* seems really transgressive against social standards. It sounds right now like Wilde picked this play to make a statement against society's conventional ideas about sex. Maybe Wilde was referring to his own role as a sexual outlaw. But I am not sure how the image of Salome can relate to his own views. I read some of Edelman's theory and Meyer's, but I am not sure how to connect it with *Salome*. This is hard to understand, and I don't know how to use it.

My response to Scott. Scott, you have found some good readings to help develop your knowledge of the play's background and interpretive perspectives. I think you are making progress in combining the roles of theater historian and dramatic interpreter. The Powell and Ellmann books will give you extensive information about the theater situation of Wilde's London and dramatic traditions he drew from. What connections are you seeing between "transgressive" physical imagery and these dramatic traditions? Do think about this connection.

Now, another issue: do you see any connection between Salome's aggressively sexual image and Wilde's own ambivalent sexual identity? If you want to apply concepts of gay identity to the "transgression" issue in *Salome,* you need to develop your knowledge of the Edelman and Meyer readings—to take on the role of queer studies theorist. I know they aren't easy reading, but they can give you a way of talking about Wilde's sense of his own transgressive identity that you won't otherwise have.

By the way, you did an important thing in your role as textual interpreter. You noticed that the website where the Tucker article came from is sponsored by a Catholic organization. As you noted, that may mean that the interests which the website represents could affect the views in the article. That doesn't devalue it, but it's an alert about how institutional interests might shape the context of an interpretation.

[I used our conference following this progress report to help Scott see that he was combining the roles of theater historian and dramatic interpreter in his project. I encouraged him to be confident that his theater background would help him understand how the theater situation of the 1890s might have shaped Wilde's plans for staging the play. At the same time, I told him I didn't find much about the implications of Wilde's own sexual identity in his progress report and that without using some theoretical issues raised by Edelman, Meyer, and others, it would be hard to read the play as a signifier of Wilde's own sexual identity. I repeated that he needed to make a choice of what interpretive roles he could best play in developing his paper.]

My interpretation of Scott's progress report. At this crucial phase, Scott had combined his interests in theater background and in dramatic analysis, to which he brought some authority as a theater major. He learned quickly about the play's composition and intended staging, and these elements together with theater history formed what I thought was a workable combination of interpretive roles. He found some good readings in 1890s theater history and dramatic influences, which helped him focus his interests in contemporary theater and dramatic patterns in the play. He also paid close attention to textual features—especially the imagery he noted as striking.

However, he ran into problems trying to assimilate the sexual-identity theories developed by Edelman and Meyer and did not pursue that approach very actively. I wanted to help him see that he needed the discursive terms of this theory if he was going to connect the theme of transgression with Wilde's own identity. But I think he saw this as a theoretical tangle he was not really prepared to unravel at this point. As I told him, I would understand if he decided to bypass this in favor of the historical/interpretive approaches he felt more confident about.

Scott's final paper

Scott's text: "Transgression in Salome.*"* Right up front, here is a major part of what I have learned from this term paper, and it may as well be my thesis: looking for an object of transgression in *Salome*—that is, something that is transgressed against—is like looking for a stalk of hay in a haystack. A stalk of hay that feels as though it should be distinctive, but isn't. Basically, my working definition of a transgression involves two ideas, one that has some kind of agreement, and another that conflicts with the first one. Most of Wilde's transgressions in *Salome* make sense, as long as viewed from a certain way. Much like a stalk of hay, viewed from the side; it is a long and thin line, but start to rotate your viewpoint around the straw, and the line gets shorter. Get in line with the straw, and it is nothing but a dot. Keep rotating, and it becomes a line again. Another distinction is transgressions that are internal and external to the play. A power structure can be transgressed against within the world of the play, or something in the play can transgress against what the play's audience may be expecting. I will try to distinguish between these perspectives in this paper.

[In this section Scott discusses various "depictions of the Salome figure in the literature of the time," then describes Wilde's composition and its first production in Paris. He introduces an interpretation that describes the play as a "symbolist" event intended to represent "the beauty of art" itself. He discounts this perspective in order to make a transition to his own interpretation of the play's imagery and dramatic structure: "I don't think that her argument that *Salome* is simply a work of art is the whole story. I think the play addresses issues of power and sexuality that Wilde wanted to deal with, and I will discuss this later in this paper."]

[In this section Scott considers the transgressive aspects of Salome's role. He begins with his image of the needle in the haystack: "Transgressions, the term I started with, are found in *Salome* like stalks of hay in a haystack." He continues by saying that when Salome kisses Iokanaan's severed head, it "is not only a transgression against Iokanaan's desires . . . but is also an internal transgression against the power structure within the play . . . a kind of victory of her passionate female sexuality over the dominant male power that Herod represents. It is altogether too dangerous, too passionate, too desirous." Scott speculates that "Wilde might be saying that Herod's power is like the power of Victorian public opinion, both must be resisted whatever the cost. Maybe Wilde was foreseeing his own destruction by showing Salome's death."]

[In this section Scott considers the implications of the climactic dance scene: "The dance seems to be a rather direct transgression of the standards for public performances in Victorian England." He says, "It reads to me as a sort of release for some of the endlessly built up passion that drives Salome, and is expressed in the transgressive imagery." The final scene intensifies in the climactic moment: "This red, intense passion takes over the entire play before it is through, presumably with lots of dripping blood on stage from the freshly severed head, and turning the moon itself red. The violent imagery itself seems a transgression against the decorum expected by theatergoers in the English public of Wilde's day."]

[Commenting on Salome's death at the end, Scott rejects the argument that "Wilde has Salome punished for her transgressions against a Catholic moral code." He says that this conclusion is simplistic and represents an interpretation promoted by (the interpreter's) religious background. Instead, "it is without doubt her passion and desire for Iokanaan's red lips that brings about her death." The ending shows "Wilde's intuition that such extremes of passion and transgression simply cannot continue to exist in a society."]

[Scott's last paragraph:] To draw all of this discussion together, bale the hay if you will, I will come back once more to my opening statement: there is a host of transgressive issues and targets in the play. Certainly much of the transgressive material revolves around passion, and some of it is clustered at certain points in the play, but they are brought to a powerful climax at the end—a theatrical bang. It is not hard to imagine why the censoring official didn't let it come out to public audiences. It would have been hard for them to handle!

My interpretation of Scott's final draft. I told Scott I liked his blend of authority in the roles of theater historian and interpreter of dramatic action. And his draft also showed his ability to do close readings of imagery, integrating his textual readings with his analyses of dramatic structure. His framing metaphor of hay and straw (he is a midwesterner, after all) seemed an effort to signify his understanding of the difficulty complexity of his topic—transgression—in a concrete way. I viewed it as a deliberate rhetorical move to convey to the reader his sense of the persistent ambiguities of the term "transgression." In this sense, while it may be strained, I saw it as his way of positioning his voice within a discursive field he recognized as uncertain and ambiguous for a novice interpreter. I also liked the way he read Salome's death in terms of the play's dramatic structure and combined it with attention to the imagery. He clearly positioned his view against the argument that her death is to be seen as moral punishment. He relied on his mastery of the play's dramatic framework to foreground the theatricality of the final scene—the "theatrical bang" phrase.

Then he added his judgment that Salome's death might show Wilde's intuition of the social cost of sexual transgression. More elaboration of this point would have strengthened the paper, but obviously during his revision process he finally decided he wasn't prepared to use sexual-identity theory from Edelman and Meyer to make any significant interpretive judgment. This choice did lessen the interpretive range of the paper, as I told him, but concentrating his focus on theater history and dramatic interpretation allowed him to build further on his existing authority and expertise. In all, I think Scott moved clearly into the rhetorical spaces of the interpretive discourses he did use, responding to other views as he constructed his own.

Building Authority as Writers: Ann and Scott

The two students in this chapter are typical of many American students as writers, bringing widely varied interests, study goals, and experience levels to any given learning/writing task. Each began work at the boundaries of the knowledge community in which his or her tasks were situated. Neither student was a major in the area represented by the course, nor did either have significant experience in the knowledge-building strategies required by the projects. They had to gain a working authority in the genres and theoretical terms required by their projects, even as they devised the rhetorical strategies needed to mediate other voices and views through the stabilizing center of their own voices. Each faced the challenge of learning to analyze and compose knowledge claims in unfamiliar discursive contexts. Ann's challenge was quite different from Scott's and required different teaching strategies in my efforts to help them develop their projects.

Family literacy study is well suited to helping inexperienced undergraduates like Ann move beyond boundary status to gain experience in basic knowledge-making strategies of literacy study. It worked well for Ann, enabling her to shape personal knowledge and family contexts within the analytic framework of studies by Brandt, Auerbach, and others I chose because I found them accessible to inexperienced readers. Classroom and small-group discussions of these studies helped Ann and the other students articulate important literacy issues. My main goals were to help Ann become familiar with the methods of interviewing, transcribing, and analyzing literacy narratives and identify important points of contact between her findings and insights from the literacy studies we had read. I saw both of these masteries as essential to Ann's feeling of active participation in the field of literacy studies. And indeed, Ann had fun interviewing her grandmothers, whose histories of origin and cultural adaptation she had known little about, and had found it striking that both she and her dad had thought of the same teacher as a "literacy mentor."

Unlike Ann, Scott had as much experience in his major as an undergraduate could have, both in onstage theater work and in drama history and interpretation. He brought a practiced actor's eye and familiarity with dramatic structure to his study of *Salome*. While my challenge with Ann was to help her gain some sense of authority in literacy study, my task with Scott was to help him adapt his strong authority as a dramatic interpreter to the challenge of textual and historical interpretation. We readily agreed on a focus on *Salome* and identified a number of useful critical readings in English comic traditions and theater history of the 1890s. But there was another, more problematic element in our discussions as well, since the text of *Salome* brought transgressive sexual issues to the fore. I saw one of my challenges as helping Scott engage the discourses of sexual-identity theory sufficiently to help him interpret Wilde's subjective presence in

Salome—to determine whether the play could be seen as Wilde's effort to inscribe his own sense of fate in dramatic form. This effort met with only modest success, however. While Scott's active participation in classroom discussions showed that he had engaged some theoretical issues, he did not feel that he had enough authority to engage this theory in an interpretive judgment in his paper. This outcome should remind us that such challenges are often only partly met and fulfilled, and opportunities to gain authority as learners and writers should be an ongoing priority for students and teachers alike.

Appendix 5.1: Family Literacy Issues

Note: This is not meant to be an outline of your paper; it is a listing of issues that you might appropriately consider if your project focuses on family literacy study.

1. What are the literacy backgrounds and histories of the family members you will focus on?

    a. What are the major characteristics of their literacy backgrounds?

    b. What are significant transitions, changes, or developments in their literacy histories?

    c. What forms of literacy did these family members ultimately develop? How did they use their literacies—in what kinds of personal development, work, family life, or community activity did their literacies come into play?

2. To what extent does your family literacy environment contain the basic literate practices described by Purcell-Gates in her chapter "A World Without Print"?

3. To what extent does your family environment reflect the connections between home and school literacy contained in the school literacy model presented in Auerbach's article?

    a. To what extent was there a positive or reinforcing connection between your family literacy environment and the school literacy requirements?

b. To what extent was there conflict or dissonance between your home and school literacy environments?

4. Were there any literacy mentors of the kind Brandt describes in her article "Sponsors of Literacy"?

5. To what extent have family members "accumulated" literacy in the sense Brandt uses the term?

6 / Building Transformative Opportunities in Institutional Contexts

Bringing Change

In educational systems, there is always space for change. How change comes about, however, depends on many factors. Often in academic institutions it develops through long-term program review and restructuring carried out by committees and administrative units. Many flourishing curricular ventures have emerged from this large-scale, time-consuming process. Indeed, this kind of change is probably easier in American postsecondary institutions than in many other countries with well-developed systems, because the American system is so decentered. For this reason, American institutions can respond to forces for change more quickly. This contrast is noticeable, for example, in the current debate in German universities about adopting four-year baccalaureate programs as alternatives to the standard master's degree. While some universities would like to develop such degree programs, the new ventures must be negotiated among multiple layers of internal and external governance at various state and federal levels in Germany before planning is finalized, and the process is still ongoing. In this comparative perspective, the American postsecondary system is more flexible and less tradition-bound, so curriculum and program changes can occur at different levels within and across institutions.

The transformative projects proposed in this book are intended to build upon existing programs and individual teachers' planning efforts. These projects can be implemented at the institutional or program level or by instructors who want to develop transformative writing opportunities in their courses. At the program level, there are several current models receptive to transformative projects, often with existing writing components readily available for strengthening. Writing-across-the- curriculum (WAC) programs, for example, come

172

in many forms, some offering support for individual instructors' attention to writing, others providing overarching writing expectations and structures for disciplinary offerings. Service learning courses and programs, which often feature self-directed writing projects as important learning elements, may also be strengthened with transformative writing opportunities. Later in this chapter I will suggest how certain specific features of transformative projects can strengthen these important programs.

Teachers on an individual basis can build opportunities for students to write transformatively as knowledge-makers, selecting the right course contexts and settings for this purpose. Teachers may plan for themselves the tasks that connect students with the opportunities—and the risks—of self-directed, goal-driven writing and knowledge-making. The planning steps suggested in chapters 4 and 5 build on what teachers in many disciplines already do, designing research papers, term papers, and final projects. Too often, however, such tasks are constrained by the inherent pressures of the American semester, limiting the cumulative, self-directed qualities that I maintain are crucial to transformative writing. The deadline-oriented pattern of most undergraduate courses may reduce students' freedom to change, shift focus, or reformulate goals as they develop their projects. The tensions between students' freedom and semester constraints must be incorporated in task structures themselves, so that students experience both the risks and the responsibilities of their choices as they develop their projects.

I believe individual teachers working within specific learning contexts can readily build opportunities for self-directed learning and writing. Yagelski says that "when it comes to substantive educational reform, small is not only beautiful but essential" because educational change "is always local" (184–85). As core agents of change, individual teachers are well able to construct the spaces in their own courses for undergraduates to learn the traits of active knowledge-makers. Students must have sufficient time and freedom to define specific issues and problems, assimilate information and ideas, and contest others' views as they reformulate their own understanding. Setting their own project goals can help students see that they have an important stake in the process, that rethinking and rewriting are not simply wheel-spinning but the means by which knowledge must be constructed. Early discussions with instructors and peers can jump-start students' thinking about their goals for a semester-long project.

With respect to the broader curricular picture for American undergraduates, one- or two-semester general education courses may leave students feeling on the borders of communities as writers and knowledge-makers. They can limit students' opportunities for in-depth, self-directed writing experiences, as the cases of the lower-level American students in this study show. In these students' introductory-level general education courses, writing components consisted of a series of short tasks effective in helping them learn major issues and texts but lacking the range of in-depth projects based on the knowledge-making strategies of specific disciplines. First-year seminars and interest groups, bolstered by extended writing projects that embed students in specific disciplinary discourses, can help offset general education's propensity for scattershot experiences. Midwestern University's first-year seminar program, for example—a one-semester requirement exemplified by Ann's course in chapter 5—seeks to give new students a strong participatory experience in a specific discipline. Such courses can be very helpful in giving students initial familiarization with disciplinary issues and discourses. The drawback of such programs is that students may have little chance for follow-up experiences in these disciplines as they continue to fulfill general education requirements. Interdisciplinary studies, the basis of many learning-community projects, can pose additional difficulties for students by necessitating activity in boundary spaces of multiple disciplines simultaneously. These factors can reduce undergraduates' ongoing participation in specific knowledge communities in their early college semesters.

Because of these pressures in the American undergraduate pattern, it is especially important for teachers across the curriculum to help students build the extended, self-directed projects that invest them in specific knowledge communities. These projects can strengthen WAC courses, service learning courses, and other activity-based academic experiences. The projects proposed in chapters 4 and 5 are especially appropriate to courses in writing-across-the-curriculum networks. The WAC movement has an extensive, powerful role in undergraduate learning in many institutions. Emerging first during a period of rapidly increasing enrollments in American institutions in the 1960s and 1970s, the WAC impetus intensified as enrollment pressures grew in traditional undergraduate composition programs. As institutions devoted more and more resources to writing instruction during this period, departments sponsoring writing programs came to believe that the question "Who should teach writing?" demanded new answers. One response—from English departments and administrators—was to begin spreading responsibility to faculty in other programs outside English departments. Economic pressures on English and composition programs were one factor in these moves, but teachers' frustration with their ways of responding to students' writing was a guiding force in WAC successes. Many faculty—including a number at Midwestern University in this study—came to believe that writing belonged at the center of learning work in their disciplines. The chance to link students' writing directly to their own disciplines appealed to faculty previously content to pigeonhole writing as the responsibility of English teachers. Faculty members in different disciplines, says Russell, began to "explore the relationships between the structure of the discipline, as revealed in its discourse, and the ways in which students learned that structure and discourse" (*Writing* 285). WAC initiatives in many institutions put into motion a cross-disciplinary energy enabling faculty to reach out to each other across existing disciplinary boundaries. The transformative model I propose in chapters 4 and 5 can augment the writing elements of courses within WAC networks.

WAC initiatives have mediated underlying tensions among competing intellectual and professional interests, enabling teachers in many knowledge fields to find common ground for connecting writing and knowledge-making. Walter Damrosch argues that interdisciplinary moves like WAC programs can "transcend both the disciplinary isolation and social disjointedness that pervade academic life" and break down the "archaic hyperindividualism" of university life (6–7). WAC groups have been effective in crossing disciplinary borders, bringing faculty together to create influential faculty-development programs and other cross-departmental collaborations that have encouraged the use of writing-based teaching strategies. The largest obstacle to success for WAC programs is the inherent competition among disciplines for the resources in the institution. And as Russell points out, WAC programs are vulnerable to the underlying tensions among disciplines, whose practitioners may distrust collaborative initiatives that require the sharing of power: "Until individual disciplines accept the responsibility of . . . the teaching of writing, WAC programs will continue to be marginalized" (*Writing* 298). Competitive tensions within a WAC program can be reduced by systematic faculty sharing of writing plans and strategies. Transformative writing projects are an ideal focus of attention for such sharing because they allow faculty members to speak to common issues from the contexts of their own disciplinary discourses.

Another initiative, based on the idea of the "learning community," has gained momentum in many institutions in recent years. It includes course clustering, interactive learning strategies, and student interest groupings. Programs based on first-year seminars and freshman interest groups have been created to bring students into groups with common interests. Like WAC programs, most of these efforts seek "greater curricular coherence, more opportunities for active learning, and interaction between students and faculty," says Barbara Leigh Smith ("Creating" 33). These learning-community initiatives—like the WAC movement itself—now face what Smith calls "classic second-stage reform issues" as programs assess their long-term impact on student learning. Many programs, says Smith, have become "little more than block registration devices, with little alteration of the teaching and learning environment" ("Challenge" 5). But along with the WAC programs, with which they are often combined, learning-community structures often include extended writing projects immersing students in specific knowledge fields. These projects can push students' writing beyond a "display of their ability to analyze and synthesize" toward writing as "'the real thing'—that is, the kind of writing practitioners in the field might be doing" (Zawacki and Williams 119).

Service learning courses often include long-term, self-directed writing projects immersing students in specific communities of practice. Two primary components of service learning, says Edward Zoltkowski, are participation in "service activities that meet actual community needs" and academic tasks that help students "think, discuss, or write about what they learned" (qtd. in Joliffe, "Writing" 88). The most popular writing task for service learning, notes Joliffe, is journal keeping, which helps students reflect on their immediate personal responses to their experiences. But though journaling allows personal reflection, Joliffe also notes that journals are not meant to give students a broad basis for perspective-building. For example, a student may reflect on her activities as a literacy tutor in her journal, but journaling may not challenge her to address issues of power relations and cultural positioning in response to broader perspectives of literacy professionals. In-depth writing projects connecting students' direct experiences with issues in the service field are essential to building authority. Internship activities in nonprofit organizations, public services, and business organizations can also give students opportunities to develop writing projects in specific fields. When they are structured as academic work, such opportunities can lead to broader perspectives on issues embedded in the specific context of the activity. As Joliffe notes, students must be more than observers on the boundaries of service or internship arenas; they must "*participate* in the activity system" as reflective insiders ("Writing" 106). This challenge to reflect as insiders requires the in-depth, issue-rich writing project that enables students to relate their own judgments to the contested issues of the field.

In many institutions, honors programs also offer opportunities for students to develop goal-driven, self-directed writing projects in specific courses and as independent thesis projects. The honors program at Midwestern University includes these features, sponsoring courses that typically require in-depth study and research leading to significant semester writing projects and offering students the opportunity to develop a thesis project as an additional challenge in their major area. These tasks require teachers' strong expectations for students. They epitomize the challenges of autonomy and self-motivation that help students learn to connect writing and knowledge-making. However, honors programs are by nature both selective and restrictive. As with Midwestern's program, most direct their strong expectations and challenges only to students they deem most capable of academic success. At Midwestern, for example, only 10 to 15 percent of the student body participate in honors work, and only a small percentage of those complete the thesis project. In the goals for change outlined below, I propose that the values associated with honors work—long-term goal-setting, self-directed planning and writing, and interactive participation in knowledge communities—be spread broadly across the undergraduate curriculum to challenge undergraduates in as many settings as possible.

Developing Change Goals

These curricular initiatives have helped teachers situate extended, self-directed writing tasks in specific communities of knowledge and practice. They offer important venues for transformative writing projects. To make best use of these opportunities, teachers and program advisers should consider the following purposes as they shape their expectations for students:

- Help students learn to set their own goals and develop their own tasks as writers and practitioners.
- Help students develop reflective, recursive planning and writing practices.
- Help students experience the relational, interactive work of knowledge-making in specific communities of knowledge and practice.

These purposes can augment and reinforce the opportunities already available in the program initiatives discussed in this chapter. The following goals for change can support this process:

Change Goal One: Develop Seminar-Like Courses

Develop variable-credit, seminar-like courses at all levels of study whose primary focus is students' own extended goal-setting/research/writing activity.

These courses should be student-centered, not coverage-centered. They should invite students into self-directed, goal-oriented activity in the genres and activities of specific knowledge fields. The courses should focus on students' inquiries, research, planning, and writing related to their own projects. These projects should involve both collaborative and individual activities to help students discover the roles of each kind of activity in the larger contexts of knowledge-making in the discipline.

Courses should be offered at various levels of credit to make them more adaptable to the needs of students and different program curricula. The scope of the writing project should correspond to the credit level. This flexibility would enhance students' opportunities to plan project-based courses that fit their program needs.

Change Goal Two: Build Extended Writing Expectations

Develop curricular expectations supporting extended, cumulative writing projects in a wide range of courses already in place in programs and disciplines.

Such expectations would recognize the crucial value of in-depth, long-term writing tasks as immersion experiences for all undergraduates in specific disciplinary or interdisciplinary communities. Students' commitment to such tasks has been shown to increase their identification with the values and motives of specific knowledge fields. Systematic expectations should support, without preempting, individual faculty planning in individual courses. Courses should be organized to encourage students to set early goals for projects, develop them over time, and engage in reflective, recursive writing and revision of texts.

Change Goal Three: Encourage Students' Self-Directed, Long-Term Planning/Writing Roles

Encourage faculty to shape students' roles as self-directed, long-term planners, researchers, and writers.

Deadline pressures built into the semester system are a key determiner of American students' authorship attitudes and writing practices.

Typical semester-deadline time structures reward students who become skilled in rapid, short-burst composing/revising. This pattern is often established in introductory courses emphasizing frequent short writing assignments. It is important for students to have alternative experiences in extended learning/writing projects that require sustained commitment to task goals.

To achieve this goal, instructors should institute cumulative, self-directed writing tasks as a basic component of course design whenever possible. Students should be responsible for sustaining goals and making choices as they shape the outcomes of their tasks. Students' proactive use of time should be instantiated in course schedules, with an emphasis on recursive stages of planning, researching, presentation/feedback, and writing/revising.

Course designs should emphasize the following:

- sufficient lead time in task formation to sustain the long-term evolution of the project
- activities that support task development: conferences, proposals, in-progress reports, presentation/peer group activities, drafting/feedback activities
- timely feedback from instructors and peers during planning, researching, and revision

Each of these goals can reinforce patterns and practices already in place in many institutions and, if expanded in institutional settings, can strengthen students' opportunities to write as knowledge-makers.

A Final Word

I began this book as a cross-national study of German and American student writers and conclude it with an argument for strengthening extended writing opportunities for all American students. Some of my readers may be situated in German institutions, but most will be American teachers and planners in a variety of disciplines who—my hope is—will find that the cross-national study in the early chapters highlights what I say about American students' writing in later chapters. Indeed, the comparisons in early chapters may tempt American readers to think I have privileged German institutions or perhaps romanticized the German academic tradition. I hope that my discussion of the shortcomings of German academic writing traditions in chapter 3 shows this to be untrue. For while I strongly value the challenges that autonomy offers German students as writers, it should be clear that I find comparative strengths in American writing pedagogy as well, especially American students' opportunities for the kind of interactive feedback during composing and revising that is unavailable to German students. I believe the most important differences between German and American students as writers are that they are tasked differently and that they respond to different expectations. My thesis in the last two chapters is that American teachers should expect more from their students as self-directed, long-term planners and writers and should construct tasks based on those expectations.

These priorities for change invite teachers' responses at both individual and program levels. However, faculty members' positions and status in their institutions, and the nature of their institutions, will strongly affect how they can respond to this invitation. In any change movement, the differences between regular appointments and part-time/temporary positions can strongly affect how faculty can bring pedagogical change. Faculty in tenure-line or returning appointments, with ongoing responsibility for courses and program planning, will have the freedom to develop or expand transformative writing projects in their own courses. Part-time and temporary instructors and teaching assistants often do not (at Midwestern University, an average of 30 percent of English studies course work is taught by temporary faculty; in many institutions, the percentage is higher, sometimes much higher). Especially in courses where individual sections are centrally planned, temporary faculty and teaching assistants have little input. For this reason, it is crucial for faculty to share decision-making power as broadly as possible. The challenge of power-sharing is a major issue in many institutions, and the transformative priorities I propose require careful, sustained planning. Only active participation by many faculty can bring the strong expectations and challenging opportunities of transformative writing in the broadest possible way to undergraduates in American colleges and universities.

Works Cited

Index

Works Cited

Adams, Katherine. *A History of Professional Writing Instruction in American Colleges.* Dallas: Southern Methodist UP, 1993.

Anweiler, Oskar. "Deutschland." *Bildungssysteme in Europa.* Ed. O. Anweiler. Weinheim: Beltz Verlag, 1996. 31–56.

Ash, Mitchell G. "Common and Disparate Dilemmas of German and American Universities." *Universities in the Twenty-first Century.* Ed. Steven Muller with Heidi L. Whitesell. Providence, RI: Berghahn, 1996. 37–48.

Aufenanger, Stefan. "Qualitativ Analyse semi-structurelle Interviews-Ein Werkstattbericht." *Qualitativ-Empirische Sozialforschung: Konzepte, Methoden, Analysen.* Opladen, Germany: Westdeutschen Verlag, 1991.

Ballenger, Bruce. *Beyond Note Cards: Rethinking the Freshman Research Paper.* Portsmouth, NH: Boynton/Cook, 1999.

Bartholomae, David. "Inventing the University." *When a Writer Can't Write: Studies in Writer's Block and Other Composing Problems.* Ed. Mike Rose. New York: Guilford, 1985. 134–65.

———. "Writing with Teachers: A Conversation with Peter Elbow." *College Composition and Communication* 46.1 (Feb. 1995): 62–71.

Bazerman, Charles. *Constructing Experience.* Carbondale: Southern Illinois UP, 1994.

Beaufort, Anne. "Learning the Trade: A Social Apprenticeship Model for Gaining Writing Expertise." *Written Communication* 17.2 (2000): 185–223.

Berlin, James. *Writing Instruction in Nineteenth-Century American Colleges.* Carbondale: Southern Illinois UP, 1984.

Bizzell, Patricia. "What Is a Discourse Community?" *Academic Discourse and Critical Consciousness.* Pittsburgh: U of Pittsburgh P, 1992. 222–37.

Brandt, Deborah. "The Cognitive as the Social: An Ethnomethodological Approach to Writing Process Research." *Written Communication* 9.3 (1992): 315–55.

Brauer, Gerd. Letter to the author. Apr. 4, 1996.

Carroll, Lee Ann. *Rehearsing New Roles: How College Students Develop as Writers.* Studies in Writing and Rhetoric. Carbondale: Southern Illinois UP, 2002.

Chin, Elaine. "Redefining 'Context' in Research on Writing." *Written Communication* 11.4 (1994): 445–82.

Clark, Romy, and Roz Ivanic. *The Politics of Writing.* London: Routledge, 1997.

Council of Writing Program Administrators. "Outcomes Statement for First-Year Students." *College English* 63 (2001): 321–25.

Crowley, Sharon. *Composition in the University.* Pittsburgh: U of Pittsburgh P, 1998.

Damrosch, Walter. *We Scholars: Changing the Culture of the University.* Cambridge: Harvard UP, 1995.

Davis, H. W. "Mastering Principles of Composition." *The English Journal* 19.10 (1930): 795–803.

Davis, Robert, and Mark Shadle. "'Building a Mystery': Alternative Research Writing and the Academic Act of Seeing." *College Composition and Communication* 51 (Feb. 2000): 417–46.

deRudder, Helmut. "Comparing German and American Higher Education: Remarks on Presentations by Gerhard Konow and Patrick Callan." *Universities in the Twenty-first Century.* Ed. Steven Muller with Heidi L. Whitesell. Providence, RI: Berghahn, 1996. 69–78.

Donahue, Tiane. "France: The Lycée-to-University Progression and French Students' Development as Writers." *Writing and Learning in Cross-National Perspective.* Ed. David Foster and David R. Russell. Urbana, IL: NCTE; Mahwah, NJ: Erlbaum, 2002. 134–91.

Dunmire, Patricia. "Genre as Temporally Situated Social Action." *Written Communication* 17.1 (2000): 93–138.

Educational Commission of the States. "States That Require Students to Pass an Assessment with a Minimum Score to Graduate." 2000 <www.ecs.org/clearinghouse/15/52/1552.html>.

Educational Testing Service. 2002 <www.collegeboard.org/ap/index.html>.

Elbow, Peter. "Being a Writer vs. Being an Academic: A Conflict in Goals." *College Composition and Communication* 46 (1995): 72–83.

———. "Reflections on Academic Discourse: How It Relates to Freshmen and Colleagues." *Negotiating Academic Literacies: Teaching and Learning Across Languages and Cultures.* Ed. Vivian Zamel and Ruth Spack. Mahwah, NJ: Erlbaum, 1998. 145–70.

Ellwein, Thomas. *Die deutsche Universität Vom Mittelalter bis zur Gegenwart.* Wiesbaden: Fourier Verlag, 1997.

Faigley, Lester. *Fragments of Rationality: Postmodernity and the Subject of Composition.* Pittsburgh: U of Pittsburgh P, 1992.

Fallon, Daniel. *The German University: A Heroic Ideal in Conflict with the Modern World.* Boulder: Colorado Associated UP, 1980.

Fischer-Appelt, Peter. "The University: Past, Present, and Future." In *Universities in the Twenty-first Century.* Ed. Steven Muller with Heidi L. Whitesell. Providence, RI: Berghahn, 1996. 3–14.

Flexner, Abraham. *Universities: American, English, German.* New York: Oxford UP, 1930.

Flower, Linda. *The Construction of Negotiated Meaning: A Social Cognitive Theory of Writing.* Carbondale: Southern Illinois UP, 1994.

———. *Learning to Rival: A Literate Practice for Intercultural Inquiry.* Mahwah, NJ: Erlbaum, 2000.

Foster, David. "Community and Cohesion in the Writing/Reading Classroom." *JAC* 17.3 (1997): 325–42.

Foster, David, and David R. Russell. *Writing and Learning in Cross-National Perspective: Transitions from Secondary to Higher Education.* Urbana, IL: NCTE; Mahwah, NJ: Erlbaum, 2002.

France, Alan W. "Dialectics of Self: Structure and Agency as the Subject of English." *College English* 63 (Nov. 2000): 145–65.

Führ, Christoph. *The German Educational System since 1945.* Bonn: Inter Nationes, 1997.

Gee, James P. *Social Linguistics and Literacies.* 2nd ed. London: Taylor and Francis, 1996.

Geisler, Cheryl. *Academic Literacy and the Nature of Expertise.* Hillsdale, NJ: Erlbaum, 1994.

Giddens, Anthony. *The Constitution of Society.* Berkeley: U of California P, 1984.

———. *Social Theory and Modern Sociology.* Stanford, CA: Stanford UP, 1987.

Golz, Reinhard, and Wolfgang Mayrhofer. *Education in Germany: An Overview of Developments in the Unification Process.* Alberta, Canada: Alberta Learning Center, 2000.

Gordon, Virginia, ed. *Issues in Advising the Undecided College Student.* The Freshman Year Experience 15. Columbia: National Resource Center for the Freshman Year Experience, University of South Carolina, 1995.

Gorzelsky, Gwen. "Ghosts: Liberal Education and Negotiated Authority." *College English* 64 (2002): 302–25.

Gosden, Christopher. *Social Being and Time.* Oxford, UK: Blackwell, 1994.

Greene, Stuart. "Making Sense of My Own Ideas: The Problems of Authorship in a Beginning Writing Classroom." *Written Communication* 12 (1995): 186–218.

Hanks, William F. Foreword. *Situated Learning: Legitimate Peripheral Participation.* By Jean Lave and Etienne Wenger. Cambridge: Cambridge UP, 1991. 13–24.

Harris, Joseph. "Revision as a Critical Practice." *College English* 65 (2003): 577–92.

———. *A Teaching Subject: Composition since 1966.* Prentice Hall Studies in Writing and Culture. Upper Saddle River, NJ: Prentice, 1997.

Herrington, Anne J., and Marcia Curtis. *Persons in Process: Four Stories of Writing and Personal Development in College.* Urbana, IL: NCTE, 2000.

Horner, Bruce. *Terms of Work for Composition: A Materialist Critique.* Albany: State U of New York P, 2000.

Joliffe, David A. *Inquiry and Genre: Writing to Learn in College.* Boston: Allyn, 1999.

———. "Writing Across the Curriculum and Service Learning." *WAC for the New Millennium: Strategies for Continuing Writing-Across-the-Curriculum Programs.* Ed. Susan H. McLeod et al. Urbana, IL: NCTE, 2001. 86–108.

Kruse, Otto, and Eva-Maria Jakobs. "Schreiben lehren an der Hochschule: Ein Überblick." *Schlüsselkompetenz Schreiben.* Ed. Otto Kruse, Eva-Maria Jakobs, and Gabriela Ruhmann. Neuwied, Germany: Luchterhand Verlag, 1999. 19–34.

LaCapra, Dominick. "Writing History, Writing Trauma." *Writing and Revising the Disciplines.* Ed. Jonathan Monroe. Ithaca, NY: Cornell UP, 2002. 147–80.

Lave, Jean, and Etienne Wenger. *Situated Learning: Legitimate Peripheral Participation.* Cambridge: Cambridge UP, 1991.

Lea, Mary R., and Brian V. Street. "Student Writing and Staff Feedback in Higher Education: An Academic Literacies Approach." *Student Writing in Higher Education.* Ed. Mary R. Lea and Barry Stierer. Buckingham, UK: Society for Research into Higher Education and Open University Press, 2000. 32–46.

Lee, Amy. *Composing Critical Pedagogies: Teaching Writing as Revision.* Urbana, IL: NCTE, 2002.

Legenhausen, Lienhard. Letter to the author. June 13, 2002.

Little, David. *Learner Autonomy: Definitions, Issues, and Problems.* Dublin: Authentik, 1991.

Maier, Charles S. *Dissolution: The Crisis of Communism and the End of East Germany.* Princeton: Princeton UP, 1997.

Martin, Rachel. *Listening Up: Reinventing Ourselves as Teachers and Students.* Portsmouth, NH: Boynton/Cook-Heinemann, 2001.

Matheson, Nancy, et al. *Education Indicators: An International Perspective.* Washington, DC: National Center for Education Statistics, 1996.

McCarthy, Lucille Parkinson, and Stephen M. Fishman. "Boundary Conversations: Conflicting Ways of Knowing in Philosophy and Interdisciplinary Research." *Research in the Teaching of English* 25 (1991): 419–67.

Moss, Beverly J. "Ethnography and Composition." *Methods and Methodology in Composition Research.* Ed. Gesa Kirsch and Patricia Sullivan. Carbondale: Southern Illinois UP, 1992.

National Association of Independent Colleges and Universities. *Independent Colleges and Universities: A National Profile.* Washington, DC: NAICU, 2004.

National Center for Educational Statistics. 2004 <http://nces.ed.gov/programs/digest/d04/tables/dt04_182.asp>.

Penrose, Ann M., and Cheryl Geisler. "Reading and Writing Without Authority." *College Composition and Communication* 45 (Dec. 1994): 505–20.

Petraglia, Joseph. "Writing as an Unnatural Act." *Reconceiving Writing, Rethinking Writing Instruction.* Ed. Joseph Petraglia. Mahwah, NJ: Erlbaum, 1995. 79–100.

Prior, Paul A. *Writing/Disciplinarity: A Sociohistoric Account of Literate Activity in the Academy.* Mahwah, NJ: Erlbaum, 1998.

Purves, Alan C., ed. *The IEA Study of Written Composition II: Education and Per-*

formance in Fourteen Countries. Vol. 6 of *International Studies in Educational Achievement.* Oxford: Pergamon, 1992.

Richardson, Mark. "Who Killed Annabel Lee? Writing about Literature in the Composition Classroom." *College English* 66 (2004): 278–93.

Rogoff, Barbara. *Apprenticeship in Thinking: Cognitive Development in Social Context.* New York: Oxford UP, 1990.

Rose, Mike. "The Language of Exclusion: Writing Instruction at the University." *Negotiating Academic Literacies: Teaching and Learning Across Languages and Cultures.* Mahwah, NJ: Erlbaum, 1998.

Rudolph, Frederick. *Curriculum: A History of the American Undergraduate Course of Study since 1636.* San Francisco: Jossey-Bass, 1977.

Russell, David R. "Activity Theory and Its Implications for Writing Instruction." *Reconceiving Writing, Rethinking Writing Instruction.* Ed. Joseph Petraglia. Mahwah, NJ: Erlbaum, 1995. 51–77.

———. "Rethinking Genre in School and Society: An Activity Theory Analysis." *Written Communication* 14.4 (1997): 504–54.

———. "Where Do the Naturalistic Studies of WAC/WID Point?" *WAC for the New Millennium: Strategies for Continuing Writing-Across-the-Curriculum Programs.* Ed. Susan H. McLeod et al. Urbana, IL: NCTE, 2001. 259–98.

———. *Writing in the Academic Disciplines.* Carbondale: Southern Illinois UP, 1991.

Shapiro, Nancy S., and Jodi H. Levine. *Creating Learning Communities.* San Francisco: Jossey-Bass, 1999.

Smith, Barbara Leigh. "The Challenge of Learning Communities as a Growing National Movement." *Peer Review* 3/4 (Fall 2001): 4–8.

———. "Creating Learning Communities." *Liberal Education* 79.4 (1993): 32–39.

Smith, Karl A., and Jean MacGregor. "Making Small-Group Learning and Learning Communities a Widespread Reality." *Strategies for Energizing Large Classes: From Small Groups to Learning Communities.* Ed. Jean MacGregor, James L. Cooper, Karl A. Smith, and Pamela Robinson. San Francisco: Jossey-Bass, 2000. 77–88.

Spellmeyer, Kurt. "A Common Ground: The Essay in the Academy." *Negotiating Academic Literacies: Teaching and Learning Across Languages and Cultures.* Ed. Vivian Zamel and Ruth Spack. Mahwah, NJ: Erlbaum, 1998.

Stake, Robert E. *The Art of Case Study Research.* Thousand Oaks, CA: Sage, 1993.

Statistisches Bundesamt Deutschland, Wiesbaden. "Studiendauer sowie Prüfungserfolgsquoten 1997 bis 2000." 2002 <www.destatis.de/themen/d/thm_bildung.php>.

Sternglass, Marilyn. *Time to Know Them: A Longitudinal Study of Writing and Learning at the College Level.* Mahwah, NJ: Erlbaum, 1997.

Street, Brian. *Social Literacies: Critical Approaches to Literacy Development, Ethnography and Education.* New York: Longman, 1995.

Swales, John M. *Other Floors, Other Voices: A Textography of a Small University Building.* Mahwah, NJ: Erlbaum, 1998.

Taylor, Warren. "Rhetoric in a Democracy." *English Journal* 27.10 (1938): 851–58.

Trimbur, John. "Agency and the Death of the Author: A Partial Defense of Modernism." *JAC* 20.2 (2000): 283–98.

———. "Consensus and Difference in Collaborative Learning." *College English* 51.6 (1989): 602–16.

Vesey, Laurence R. *The Emergence of the American University.* Chicago: U of Chicago P, 1965.

Vygotsky, Lev. *Mind in Society.* Cambridge: Harvard UP, 1978.

Wallace, David L., and Helen Rothschild Ewald. *Mutuality in the Rhetoric and Composition Classroom.* Studies in Writing and Rhetoric. Carbondale: Southern Illinois UP, 2000.

Walvoord, Barbara E., and Lucille Parkinson McCarthy. "The Future of WAC." *College English* 58 (1996): 58–78.

———. *Thinking and Writing in College.* Urbana, IL: NCTE, 1991.

White, Edward M., William D. Lutz, and Vera Kamusikiri, eds. *Assessment of Writing: Politics, Policies, Practices.* New York: MLA, 1996.

Windolf, Peter. *Die Expansion der Universitäten 1870–1985.* Stuttgart: Enke, 1990.

Wolff, Robert Paul. *The Ideal of the University.* Boston: Beacon, 1969.

Yagelski, Robert P. *Literacy Matters: Writing and Reading the Social Self.* New York: Teachers College, 2000.

Yancey, Kathleen Blake. *Reflection in the Writing Classroom.* Logan: Utah State UP, 1998.

Yin, Robert K. *Applications of Case Study Research.* Applied Social Methods Research Series. Newbury Park, CA: Sage, 1993.

———. *Case Study Research: Design and Methods.* Thousand Oaks, CA: Sage, 1994.

Zawacki, Terry Myers, and Ashley Taliaferro Williams. "Is It Still WAC? Writing Within Interdisciplinary Learning Communities." *WAC for the New Millennium: Strategies for Continuing Writing-Across-the-Curriculum Programs.* Ed. Susan H. McLeod et al. Urbana, IL: NCTE, 2001. 109–40.

Zerubavel, Eviatar. *Hidden Rhythms: Schedules and Calendars in Social Life.* Chicago: U of Chicago P, 1981.

Zimmerman, Barry J., and Andrew S. Paulsen. "Self-Monitoring During Collegiate Studying: An Invaluable Tool for Academic Self-Regulation." *Understanding Self-Regulated Learning.* New Directions for Teaching and Learning 63. Hoboken: Jossey-Bass, 1995. 13–28.

Index

Abitur, 18, 24, 31–32; as preparation for university writing, 32–33
activity system as analytic model in cross-national writing study, 35–36
Adams, Katharine, 10
agency: interpretive, 117; as knowledge-making power, 123, 129; for student writers, 7, 22, 25, 37
Anweiler, Oskar, 17, 29
apprenticeship model for undergraduate writers, 117–18
Ash, Mitchell G., 7
Aufenanger, Stefan, 42
authority for student writers: and expertise, 121–22; Jill's interpretation of, 96–97; and knowledge-making, 126–27; rhetorical, 18, 20, 102, 109; situational, 18, 65
authorship practices: in cross-national perspective, xviii, 6, 16, 25–27; rhetorical perspectives, 93–109; temporal perspectives, 60–93
autonomy for student writers: in cross-national perspective, xvi–xvii, 17–19, 33–39, 61–65, 110, 129, 181; definition of, 25–27; for German students, 5, 20–23, 33

Ballenger, Bruce, 122, 124, 137
Bartholomae, David, 106, 118, 119, 135
Bazerman, Charles, xvi, 122, 135
Beaufort, Anne, xviii
Berlin, James, 10

Bizzell, Patricia, 118
Brauer, Gerd, 20

Carroll, Lee Ann, 10–11, 14
case studies: and disciplines, 39, 47; and institutions, 44–46; and interview questions, 53–59; observer/participant role in, 42–44; and participating students, 46–53
case study framework: "pattern-matching" strategy of, 44; qualitative model of, 38–9; triangulation of, 41–42
Chin, Elaine, 36, 61
Clark, Romy, 37
Council of Writing Program Administrators, 128
Crowley, Sharon, 12
curricular change goals, 178–80
Curtis, Marcia, 10, 107, 125

Davis, H. W., 10
Davis, Robert, 103, 137–38
deadline-driven vs. goal-driven writing patterns, xvii, 2, 16, 61–66, 91–93, 110–14
deRudder, Helmut, 7
Donahue, Tiane, 21
Dunmire, Patricia, 61

Educational Commission of the States, 4
Educational Testing Service, 4
Elbow, Peter, 123
Ellwein, Thomas, 22, 45

examinations, high-stakes written, 3–5

expertise: as "great divide," 14; students' development of, 14–15, 120–24

Ewald, Helen Rothschild, 116–17, 125, 131

Faigley, Lester, 25

Fallon, Daniel, 7, 45

first-year seminars and transformative writing projects, 174–76

Fischer-Appelt, Peter, 32

Fishman, Stephen M., 13, 16, 118, 123, 136

Flexner, Abraham, 7

Flower, Linda, 116, 130, 133–34

Foster, David, 3, 63, 118

France, Alan W., 123, 127

free-time writing as German practice, 61–65

Führ, Christoph, 17, 29

Gee, James P., 36, 118

Geisler, Cheryl, 14, 104, 121, 124, 136, 156

general education: and American composition, 7, 9–17; and students' writing development, 33–35, 110, 120, 174

genre studies and cross-national writing study, 35–36, 60–61

Giddens, Anthony, xvii, 60

Golz, Reinhard, 29, 31

Gorzelsky, Gwen, 14–15

Gosden, Christopher, 61

Greene, Stuart, 13

Hanks, William F., 8

Harris, Joseph, 113, 119

Herrington, Anne J., 10, 107, 125

high-stakes written examinations, 3–5

Horner, Bruce, xxiii, 25

Ivanic, Roz, 37

Joliffe, David A., 137, 177

Kamusikiri, Vera, 27

knowledge communities, students' authority in, 117–20

LaCapra, Dominick, 104

Lave, Jeanne, 117–18

Lea, Mary R., 36–37

lecture and lecture-free periods in German universities, 63–65

Legenhausen, Lienhard, xxiii, 21

Levine, Jodi H., 118

literacy testing in American education, 4–5

Little, David, 26

Lutz, William D., 27

Maier, Charles S., xiv

Martin, Rachel, 113

Matheson, Nancy, xvi

Mayrhofer, Wolfgang, 29, 31

McCarthy, Lucille Parkinson, 13, 16, 118, 123, 126, 136

Moss, Beverly J., 38, 41, 43

National Association of Independent Colleges and Universities, 63

National Center for Educational Statistics, 9, 17

naturalistic research perspective, xv–xvi, 41–42

New Literacy Studies, 36–38

Paulsen, Andrew S. 25

Penrose, Ann M., 124

Petraglia, Joseph, 12
planning goals for teachers, 131–37
Prior, Paul, xvii, 35–36
project-based course models, 137–71
Purves, Alan, 8

revision studies and transformative
    writing, 112–17
rhetorical stance in cross-national per-
    spective, 93–106
Richardson, Mark, 125
Rogoff, Barbara, 117
Rose, Mike, 11
Rudolph, Frederick, 7
Russell, David R., xxiii, 3, 7, 12–13, 35,
    63, 126, 175–76

service learning and transformative
    writing, 176–77
Shadle, Mark, 103, 137–38
Shapiro, Nancy S., 118
short-burst writing, xix–xx, 16, 88–89,
    91–92, 107–9, 111–14
Smith, Barbara Leigh, 176
Spellmeyer, Kurt, 105
Stake, Robert E., 38, 42
Statistiches Bundesamt, 63
Sternglass, Marilyn, 10, 13, 16, 115,
    120, 126
Street, Brian V., 36–37
student interest groups, 176
Swales, John M., 61

Taylor, Warren, 10

temporal patterns in student writing:
    and graduation pressures, 62–63;
    institutional differences in, 61; in-
    stitutional calendars and, 64–65;
    and time and task duration tables,
    78, 87, 88, 89
transformative writing priorities, 126–
    30
transition from high school to univer-
    sity: and American students, 16;
    cross-national comparison of,
    xvi–xvii, 8–9, 32; and German
    students, 20–22
Trimbur, John, xvii–xviii, 118

Vesey, Laurence R., 7
Vygotsky, Lev, 122

Wallace, David L., 116–17, 125, 131
Walvoord, Barbara E., 13, 126
Wenger, Etienne, 117–18
White, Edward M., 27
Williams, Ashley Taliaferro, 176
Windolf, Peter, 7
Wissenschaft tradition, 20–21, 106
writing-across-the-curriculum (WAC),
    xxi, 111, 137, 173, 174–76

Yagelski, Robert P., 127, 173
Yin, Robert K., 40, 44

Zawacki, Terry Myers, 176
Zerubavel, Eviatar, 60, 65
Zimmerman, Barry J., 25

An emeritus professor of English at Drake University, David Foster served as the Director of Freshman Composition, Writing Workshop Director, and Associate Dean of Arts and Sciences. Foster was also a Fulbright Senior Scholar in Germany at the University of Münster and at the University of Dresden. His publications include *A Primer for Writing Teachers: Theories, Issues, Problems* and *Writing and Learning in Cross-National Perspective: Transitions from Secondary to Higher Education,* coedited with David R. Russell.

Other Books in the Studies in Writing & Rhetoric Series

*African American Literacies Unleashed: Vernacular English
and the Composition Classroom*
Arnetha F. Ball and Ted Lardner

Rhetoric and Reality: Writing Instruction in American Colleges, 1900–1985
James A. Berlin

Writing Instruction in Nineteenth-Century American Colleges
James A. Berlin

Something Old, Something New: College Writing Teachers and Classroom Change
Wendy Bishop

The Variables of Composition: Process and Product in a Business Setting
Glenn J. Broadhead and Richard C. Freed

Audience Expectations and Teacher Demands
Robert Brooke and John Hendricks

*Archives of Instruction: Nineteenth-Century Rhetorics, Readers,
and Composition Books in the Unites States*
Jean Ferguson Carr, Stephen L. Carr, and Lucille M. Schultz

Rehearsing New Roles: How College Students Develop as Writers
Lee Ann Carroll

*Dialogue, Dialectic, and Conversation: A Social Perspective
on the Function of Writing*
Gregory Clark

Toward a Grammar of Passages
Richard M. Coe

A Communion of Friendship: Literacy, Spiritual Practice, and Women in Recovery
Beth Daniell

Embodied Literacies: Imageword and a Poetics of Teaching
Kristie S. Fleckenstein

Writing Groups: History, Theory, and Implications
Anne Ruggles Gere

Sexuality and the Politics of Ethos in the Writing Classroom
Zan Meyer Gonçalves

Computers & Composing: How the New Technologies Are Changing Writing
Jeanne W. Halpern and Sarah Liggett

Teaching Writing as a Second Language
Alice S. Horning

Revisionary Rhetoric, Feminist Pedagogy, and Multigenre Texts
Julie Jung

Women Writing the Academy: Audience, Authority, and Transformation
Gesa E. Kirsch

Invention as a Social Act
Karen Burke LeFevre

A New Perspective on Cohesion in Expository Paragraphs
Robin Bell Markels

Response to Reform: Composition and the Professionalization of Teaching
Margaret J. Marshall

Gender Influences: Reading Student Texts
Donnalee Rubin

The Young Composers: Composition's Beginnings in Nineteenth-Century Schools
Lucille M. Schultz

Multiliteracies for a Digital Age
Stuart A. Selber

*Technology and Literacy in the Twenty-First Century:
The Importance of Paying Attention*
Cynthia L. Selfe

Language Diversity in the Classroom: From Intention to Practice
Edited by Geneva Smitherman and Victor Villanueva

Whistlin' and Crowin' Women of Appalachia: Literacy Practices since College
Katherine Kelleher Sohn

Across Property Lines: Textual Ownership in Writing Groups
Candace Spigelman

Personally Speaking: Experience as Evidence in Academic Discourse
Candace Spigelman

Self-Development and College Writing
Nick Tingle

Mutuality in the Rhetoric and Composition Classroom
David L. Wallace and Helen Rothschild Ewald

Evaluating College Writing Programs
Stephen P. Witte and Lester Faigley

*Minor Re/Visions: Asian American Literacy Narratives
as a Rhetoric of Citizenship*
Morris Young